*A
Harlequin
Romance*

OTHER
Harlequin Romances
by ISOBEL CHACE

- 935—A HOUSE FOR SHARING
- 1152—A GARLAND OF MARIGOLDS
- 1216—ORANGES AND LEMONS
- 1250—THE SAFFRON SKY
- 1306—A HANDFUL OF SILVER
- 1334—THE DAMASK ROSE
- 1390—SUGAR IN THE MORNING
- 1436—THE DAY THE RAIN CAME DOWN
- 1477—THE LAND OF THE LOTUS EATERS
- 1506—THE FLOWERING CACTUS
- 1561—HOME IS GOODBYE
- 1586—TO MARRY A TIGER
- 1618—THE WEALTH OF THE ISLANDS
- 1653—THE TARTAN TOUCH
- 1673—A PRIDE OF LIONS
- 1698—CADENCE OF PORTUGAL
- 1721—THE FLAMBOYANT TREE

Many of these titles are available at your local bookseller, or through the Harlequin Reader Service.

For a free catalogue listing all available Harlequin Romances, send your name and address to:

HARLEQUIN READER SERVICE,
M.P.O. Box 707, Niagara Falls, N.Y. 14302
Canadian address: Stratford, Ontario, Canada.

or use order coupon at back of book.

THE HOUSE OF THE SCISSORS

by

ISOBEL CHACE

HARLEQUIN BOOKS   TORONTO WINNIPEG

Original hard cover edition published in 1972
by Mills & Boon Limited.

© Isobel Chace 1972

SBN 373-01750-2

Harlequin edition published January 1974

All the characters in this book have no existence outside the imagination of the Author, and have no relation whatsoever to anyone bearing the same name or names. They are not even distantly inspired by any individual known or unknown to the Author, and all the incidents are pure invention.

The Harlequin trade mark, consisting of the word HARLEQUIN and the portrayal of a Harlequin, is registered in the United States Patent Office and in the Canada Trade Marks Office.

Printed in Canada

Madaka ya nyamba ya zisahani
Sasa walalive wana ya nyuni.

Where once the porcelain stood in
  the wall niches
Now wild birds nestle their fledglings.

> A Swahili poet, referring to the vanished glories of Pate, one of the ruined cities of the East African coast, in 1815.

CHAPTER ONE

ARABELLA BURNETT surveyed her grubby jeans and thin cotton shirt with a certain satisfaction. She had had enough of high fashion for a few hours. The day had been unbearably hot, without any sign of the cooling breeze that she had come to expect, blowing in off the Indian Ocean and stirring the steamy heat of the equatorial coast. All the girls had wilted in the crisp dresses they had been modelling and even the photographers, normally indifferent to anything but the picture in their lens, had said that the conditions were intolerable.

"Smile, Arab! Come on, girl! That's the peach of a dress you're wearing! Show it off, can't you? No, I see you can't! Duckie, you've only had it on ten minutes and you look as though you've slept in it! Haven't you ever heard that ladies only glow? Well, you're no lady, my pet! That dress is a mess!"

Arabella sighed. At least she didn't have to care if her shirt was grimed with sweat. Her shirt was her own and not on show, to be photographed and demonstrated in any number of glossy brochures that advertised the latest off-the-peg fashions from some of the cheaper manufacturers.

"Cheer up, Arab, it may never happen!"

Arabella started and then smiled. "It already has! Every one of those dresses will have to be washed and ironed before tomorrow. Let's hope the breeze is back then."

"I don't know," her fellow model, a girl called Jill Henderson, muttered. "We have a glorious free afternoon on the strength of it!"

Arabella grinned, well pleased herself with the

outcome. "What are you going to do with it?" she asked Jill.

"Nothing," the other girl answered, surprised that she should ask. "I'm going to lie on my bed, with the air-conditioning going flat out, and preferably without one bit of flesh touching another, and I'm going to sleep the sleep of the just!"

Arabella chuckled. "You're too lazy to be true!" she accused Jill mildly.

"And you're too scruffy to be true!" Jill retorted. "Where are you going, dressed like that?"

"Out," Arab said briefly. "I'm going for a drive in the Mini-Moke. We've barely had time to see anything since we've been here. I can hardly believe that we're really here, so I'm off to convince myself by seeing all the local sights!"

"I'd come with you," Jill offered, yawning, "but I can hardly stay awake. You'll have to tell me all about it tonight. Don't get lost, honey! And, whatever you do, don't get yourself kidnapped by the slave trade!"

Arab grinned happily. "I don't suppose I shall," she murmured amiably. "Such horrors have long since faded away into oblivion—"

"If you say so!" Jill drawled. "But I shall stay close to the hotel and the people I know!"

Arab didn't mind in the least being on her own. She was never lonely. She enjoyed her work, but she knew she would never hit the heights in modelling. She had the figure for it; she even had a quaint, piquant beauty that the cameras picked up; but she had no burning ambition and she was quite incapable of taking fashion seriously enough for it to be the most important thing in the world for her. She liked the bantering, jealous, even petty atmosphere that surrounded her, but she had always reserved areas of her time and personality for other things, private things, that consisted of dreams of what she would eventually do with her life and filling her head with innumerable pieces of useless information about anything and everything that appealed to her.

She came out of the hotel and crossed the road to where the cars were parked. There was nobody about except for two African women, naked to the waist, surrounded by their numerous children. They sat in the shade of a mango tree, idly gossiping the afternoon away. One of them lifted a hand in greeting as they saw Arab coming towards them. "*Jambo!*" they said in unison, and giggled shyly at their own impertinence.

"*Jambo*," Arab repeated. So much for fashion, she thought, as one of the women stood up, stretched herself, re-knotting her *kanga* more tightly about her, with an easy, loose-limbed movement that made their efforts of the morning seem positively inhibited as well as unnecessary.

Arab liked driving the Mini-Moke. She sat on the side and swung her long legs in, swivelling her bottom on to the driving seat as she switched on the ignition key. The engine came to life at a touch, and she reversed easily, wondering whether to turn right and explore the small town of Malindi itself, or to turn left and see what lay beyond the river that she had caught sight of previously. The call of the unknown won, and she turned left, away from Malindi, and headed up the coast in search of adventure.

It was scarcely a week since she had hurried home from the agency, hugging herself with glee, because she had been one of the models chosen to go to the tropical coastline of East Africa, which someone had decided would make a suitable backdrop for that year's summer fashions. Mombasa had been considered and rejected for some unknown reason, and the powers that be had selected Malindi as the best place for the unit to stay and work.

On arrival, they had found that Malindi was a natural harbour because of the break in the coral reef that ran up alongside the coast. It meant that, whereas almost everywhere else there were miles of silver sands and calm blue seas, at Malindi itself the sand was muddied by the unchecked ocean and the sediment brought down from the interior by the river. The fishing was good, but the photography sessions had had to be held a few miles down the coast, off Casuarina Point, where the magnificent coral gardens are now part of a maritime national park, and where the scenery was so gorgeous that everyone had sighed with satisfaction and pronounced it worth the thousands of miles they had come to find it.

But the three-mile daily journey had made it necessary to hire a fleet of cars to transport them and their luggage back and forth from the hotel and, because the company was a pleasant one to work for, doing all that it could to make the trip an enjoyable as well as profitable one, the cars had been made available for them all to use when they weren't working, provided they paid for the petrol they used and didn't race them up and down the Malindi–Mombasa highway, the only good road round about.

Actually the metal surface went a little way beyond Malindi, as far as the modern bridge that crossed the river, looking as though it had been built from a huge Meccano set. It was only after that that it fell into ruts and finally the surface gave out altogether to be replaced by corrugated, sun-baked mud, covered by a thin layer of dust that rose and fell every time a vehicle passed along it.

Arab hesitated on the bridge, looking down at the brown waters of the river below. She could imagine the crocodiles that she knew lived there snapping at her heels in an unguarded moment and shivered involuntarily. She preferred the dry land, the fields of cotton, the huge dark mango trees, the bright green of the banana trees, and the citrus trees. Best of all, she liked the eccentric shape of the pawpaw trees, with their long, thin trunks crowned by a fringe of leaves.

She had not gone much farther when she caught sight of an Arab town, below the road, that enticed her to go and take a closer look at it. The signpost told her that this was Mambrui, a town known to the Portuguese as Quilimanci. Intrigued, she followed the road down the hill and through the narrow streets that divided the small, square brown houses from one another, and out again to a space beside the sea. Immediately, half a dozen boys surrounded the Mini-Moke, all of them with broad grins that broke up the smooth blackness of their faces.

"Deutsch? English?" they asked her. "*Memsahib*, I speak English very well! Please, *memsahib*, I will show you Mambrui?"

Arab chose one of the older boys to the noisy disapproval of all the others, but he looked more reliable than the others, some of whom could barely have been in their teens.

"I am very good guide," her chosen boy informed her complacently. "I show you everything! Many tourists come here to see our town. Have you been here before?"

Arab shook her head. "I was in England last week," she told him.

He was suitably impressed. "This town has only a thousand people here now," he began in a sing-song voice. "It is a wholly Muslim town—very conservative, you understand? These are the streets. That is a shop where you can buy tea and sugar." He paused in the doorway to allow her to peer in through the door. "Do you wish to see the mosque?"

She did, so he led her there next. It turned out to be a delightful piece of Arab-rococo architecture, and she remembered having seen the minaret from the road. Now she was nearer to it, she could see the way it was decorated with cut-outs of the crescent moon and the stars, and covered with painted verses from the Koran in the free-flowing Arabic script that lends itself so well to decoration. Next door to the mosque was the Koranic school, where the children learned to recite their scriptures by heart, as well as all the legal and moral precepts laid down by the Prophet.

"Do you like Mambrui better than Malindi?" the boy asked her.

"I like them both," she answered pacifically.

"We are more religious in Mambrui," he stated unanswerably. He hesitated, obviously assessing her in his mind. "We have a holy man buried here," he said. "Do you want to see?"

Arab tried to look enthusiastic. She did not much want to see the tomb, but nor did she want to bring to an end their stroll through the streets of this romantic, if rather run-down, little town. She was enjoying looking at the people as they strolled along, the men in long white robes, their heads covered with red or white skull-caps, the women totally hidden by their all-enveloping black veils. Only the children, in their ragged Western dress, looked wholly African. Their elders had taken on the mannerisms as well as the attitudes of their medieval conquerors. They spoke Swahili, but their thoughts were moulded to the Arabic cadences of the Koran.

They passed an old man sitting on his doorstep, telling his beads, and Arab smiled at him hopefully. The old man frowned and shouted something to the boy at her side. The boy jerked his head and shrugged his shoulders, his lower lip jutting sulkily.

"What did he say?" Arab asked him.

"Nothing. He is a fool. He doesn't like visitors coming to Mambrui. We all know him well!"

Arab looked back to where the old man was sitting. "I shouldn't like to offend anyone," she began. "Perhaps I ought to go away?"

"Oh no, *memsahib*! I have told you, he is an old man. Nobody pays any attention to him these days!"

Arab wondered again what the old man had called out, but she soon forgot him as they reached a building, more elaborate than most of the ones she had seen, which housed the tomb of the holy man. There was no glass in the windows and she was able to look inside to where the elaborately carved wooden coffin was laid. The workmanship was superb and she wanted to go closer to see it the better.

"May one go in?" she asked.

The boy nodded eagerly, giving her an impatient push through the door. "Go in, go in!" he echoed.

The door swung open at her touch and she took a step into the cool interior, looking about her eagerly. No sooner had she done so than it seemed that a whole crowd of people had gathered in the doorway, led by the old man, who was shouting angrily at her guide. Arab came hastily out again and was annoyed when the old man seized her by the arm, pointing ferociously at her feet.

Arab pulled her arm away from him, rubbing the place where he had held her.

"What's the matter? What have I done wrong?" she asked of anyone who would listen. Nobody did.

She watched with horror as the boy who had been her guide threw a punch at another boy and, before she could say anything at all, everyone was doing battle with everyone else, while the old man shouted imprecations at the lot of them.

"Psst!"

Arab shot round to face whoever had addressed her. A tow-headed European child, dressed in jeans and a T-shirt, beckoned imperiously to her.

"Come away—*quick*!" the child commanded.

"But I can't just leave them to it!" Arab objected.

"You'd better!" the child advised grimly. "Come on, or we'll both get into trouble. Lucien will be absolutely furious!"

Arab felt a small hand on her arm that tugged her away from the scene of battle with surprising strength. A look over her shoulder convinced her that there was nothing she could do to stop the fighting, so she took to her heels and ran after the child as fast as she could go. They tore through the narrow streets and round the edge of the town by the sea. The child took a gigantic leap off a wall, landing in the dry sand, which was too high up for the sea to ever reach. The child sat down hard and collapsed into giggles.

"Oh, that was fun!" she claimed. "You ought to have seen your face!"

Arab stood on the edge of the beach, feeling dejected. "I don't know what went wrong!" she wailed.

The child grinned up at her. "Don't you? Don't you, really?"

Arab shook her head. She sat down beside the child, wondering if it were a boy or a girl. Perhaps the child's name would tell her.

"Do you live here?" she asked tentatively.

The child threw a stone into the encroaching sea. A flick of the fingers took it feet farther than Arab could have thrown it. A little boy, she decided.

"No," the child said simply. "I live with Lucien."

"Near here?" Arab prompted her.

The child stared at her thoughtfully. "Fairly near." The eyes stayed on Arab's face for a long moment without blinking. "I don't want to tell you exactly because Lucien doesn't like being interrupted when he's working. I came on the bus and I don't think he'd be very pleased if he knew."

"I see," Arab said gravely. "So we're both in trouble."

"You're not in trouble!" the child scoffed. "Grown-ups can do as they like. Lucien says so."

"Ye-es, but the Mini-Moke I came in is back there, in the centre of the town."

The child giggled. "If we wait long enough we can go back and get it. The bus home has gone anyway. I missed it because I was watching you." The unblinking stare was turned on Arabella again. "Most people have pretty clothes on when they stay down at the coast, but yours are *terrible*. Are they the only ones you've got?"

Arab flushed. "No," she admitted. "These are comfortable and—and practical for getting about."

"Lucien doesn't like women to wear trousers!"

"I don't care what he likes!" Arab said crossly.

"I do," the child said. "Will you take me home in the Mini-Moke? I've never driven in one. They look super! I wonder why they paint them to look like zebras?"

"I imagine it appeals to the tourists," Arab suggested. "What's your name? Mine is Arabella Burnett, but my friends call me Arab."

The child collapsed into outrageous laughter. "I must tell Lucien that!" it chuckled. "It will be worth his being cross with me! Let's go and get the Moke straight away and go home!"

Arab rose to her feet uncertainly. "You haven't told me your name," she reproved the child, wondering what the joke was.

"Hilary," the child supplied with distaste.

"That's an unusual name for a boy," Arab said encouragingly. "Hilary what?"

"Hilary Dark. I'm not a boy, I'm a girl. That's surprised you, hasn't it? I look like a boy, don't I? Lucien says I won't for much longer, *worse luck*! Boys can do all sorts of things by themselves, but girls can't. Lucien says girls are far more trouble!"

"That's because he's a man," Arab said definitely.

Hilary grinned. "Shall I tell him that? He'll think you're awfully impertinent," she added with satisfaction. "I don't think I will tell him, because he might not agree to my going out with you in the Mini-Moke, and I want to. Do you go out every day?"

"When I'm not working—"

Hilary's face fell. "I didn't know you worked. Can you be disturbed when you're working? Can I watch you?"

"I don't see why not," Arab said. "I model clothes. You could watch them taking the photographs if you like, as long as you didn't interrupt them in the middle of a shot. You'd better ask this Lucien of yours if you can come."

"Can I?" Hilary looked thoroughly pleased at the prospect. "Lucien will want to see you first." She hesitated. "Perhaps we could call in at your hotel on the way home?" she suggested carefully.

"No, my pet, we couldn't! Your Lucien can take me as I am, or not at all!"

Hilary sighed. "I'm afraid it will be not at all."

Arab looked down at her cotton shirt, stained with rust-coloured dirt, and her long legs encased in figure-hugging jeans that were frayed to her knees. Perhaps the unknown Lucien wouldn't approve of her if he were so fussy. But much she cared! She liked the ragged look and he would just have to put up with it!

"Perhaps I won't approve of him," she suggested with bravado.

Hilary looked shocked. "Everyone approves of Lucien," she said. "Women never leave him alone. That's why he doesn't like them. The only women he likes are dead ones, like Cleopatra and Queen Dido, only he says her real name was Elissa, and Sappho. He likes them because they can't answer back. Sappho was a genius," she added inconsequentially. "Lucien says so."

Arab was rather tired of Lucien's opinions by this time. "What about Dido and Cleopatra?" she asked.

Hilary considered the question carefully. "Cleopatra was clever," she acknowledged after a time. "At least I think she was. Though I don't much like Julius Caesar or Mark Antony, do you?"

Arab had to admit that she didn't, and that she didn't think she could ever have been even the teeniest bit in love with either of them.

"It's funny, isn't it?" Hilary remarked. "Dead men aren't at all interesting. I wonder why dead women are?"

Arab suppressed a smile. "Perhaps Lucien likes dead men too, if he's interested in history."

"He *lives* history," Hilary corrected her. "He makes it sound like a fairy story. We're doing the *Thousand*

and One Nights at the moment, and he's telling me the real history that lies behind them. He reads one of the stories every night before I go to sleep."

Arab, who had not known that any history lay behind the stories, thought that Lucien couldn't be quite as bad as she had imagined him. "There's some music that is all about Shahrazad," she told Hilary.

"I'll tell Lucien," the child said agreeably. "He says that the stories were some filibuster! He says it's absolutely typical of a woman to choose her tongue as a weapon to put off what's coming to her. He says—"

"Never mind what he says!" Arab interrupted hastily. "Don't you ever talk to anyone else?"

"We-ell, I talk to Ayah, but she doesn't understand much of what I say. And now I'm talking to you!"

Arab grinned. "So you are!" she commented. "Though it feels more like a relayed conversation with Lucien to me!"

Hilary eyed her reproachfully. "Don't you like talking to me?" she demanded.

"Very much!" Arab responded promptly. "Who is Ayah?"

Hilary shrugged her thin shoulders. "She looks after me. She looks after me at home too. She doesn't like being here because everyone laughs at her Swahili and they pretend that they can't understand her. She doesn't speak English very well either." She bounced up and down on a springy tussock of grass in the sand. "Shall we go and get the Mini-Moke now?" she cajoled.

Arab took a careful look over the wall and was relieved to see that there was nobody in sight. "All right," she said.

"We'll run!" Hilary shouted, suiting the action to the word.

"No, we won't!" Arab retorted sharply. "We'll walk. And we'll get in quietly and drive away as quickly as possible."

"Very cool!" Hilary chuckled. But she calmed down and walked soberly along beside Arab almost the whole

17

way to the Mini-Moke, only breaking into a run when her excitement at actually riding in such a vehicle became too much for her.

To Arabella's relief, no one appeared to notice them as they slid in over the sides of the car and she started up the engine. It was just as if she had never walked through the narrow, mud-coloured streets, as though she had never been the cause of that sudden inexplicable enmity between the old man and her guide, which had ended in that terrible fight.

She drove the car up the rutted road, rejoining the main road that led back to Malindi.

"You'll have to tell me where you live, you know," she said to Hilary. "Which way do we go?"

"Back to Malindi," Hilary directed. "We live in an old house overlooking the port. I'll show you. Lucien calls it the Villa Tanit, because he thinks the Carthaginians were here ages ago—long before Vasco da Gama, whose cross you can see from our windows."

Arab said nothing. She sped along the road towards Malindi, putting her foot hard down on the accelerator, amused by Hilary's sublime joy in speed and the feel of the hot wind in her ridiculously fair hair.

"Is Lucien fair?" she asked suddenly.

Hilary looked surprised. "No, he has black hair. What colour do you call yours?" she added. "I mean," she went on, in case she should be thought to be criticising her new friend, "my hair is yellow, isn't it? But I wouldn't call yours brown, would you? It changes when the sun gets on it."

"How about auburn?" Arab suggested dryly.

"I thought that was red," Hilary returned, unperturbed. "I wouldn't call your hair *red*! I'll ask Lucien what colour he'd call it!"

"I don't suppose he'll be interested," Arab warned her. "There's my hotel. Where do we go from here?"

"Straight on," Hilary told her. "You go past the shops. I'll tell you when to turn off." She leaned forward, concentrating on the road ahead. "You go round by the harbour. We can stop and look at the boats, if you like."

"Another time," Arab suggested. "Let's get you home first today. Your people may have missed you and be worried."

"Lucien never worries. Only he might get angry if he thinks I've gone out with you without asking first. It's something to do with being a girl, because he wouldn't care if I were grown up. He says women live on trouble and it's no good trying to keep them out of it because they love it really—"

"What about your mother?" Arab asked indignantly.

Hilary laughed tolerantly. "She's always in trouble! Lucien says that one of these days she'll be murdered in her bed and it will serve her right for poking her nose in where it's not wanted! He says dead people are much better in that respect."

Arab felt a burning sense of injustice on behalf of Mrs. Dark. She was quite certain that she wasn't going to like Lucien at all!

"How horrid of him!" she exclaimed.

Hilary's look rebuked her. "Lucien is never horrid," she said awfully. "We love him very much! My mother wouldn't be an anthropologist if it weren't for him! He—he's one in a million!"

"He must be!" Arab said.

Hilary's eyes shone with tears. "He is! He is! You'll see!"

A little shaken by the strength of her young friend's devotion to the unknown Lucien, Arab diplomatically changed the subject by pointing out Vasco da Gama's cross. "We must be near your home now," she said.

"It isn't my home. Lucien is only living there for a couple of years. I'm staying with him for a few months." She recovered her spirits suddenly, pointing up a narrow drive, edged with flowering shrubs. "It's up there! And oh, look, Lucien is in the garden!"

Hardly waiting for Arab to bring the Mini-Moke to a stop beside the large, glossy car that was already

19

standing in the drive, Hilary jumped out with an excited cry, making a rush towards the man who had turned towards them at the sound of the tyres crunching on the pebbled surface of the drive.

Arab had the impression of a tall man, black-haired and strong-looking, whose unsmiling gaze disconcerted her and made her bitterly conscious of her ragged clothes. She got reluctantly out of the Mini-Moke, stooping to re-tie the thong of one of her sandals to give herself time to recover her usual self-confidence and for the colour to subside out of her cheeks.

"Well, Hilary?" the man prompted the little girl.

"This is a friend of mine," Hilary said in a curious, off-hand manner. "She's come to have tea with us."

Arab stood up, summoning up a smile. "I hope you don't mind, Mr. Dark—"

"My name is Lucien Manners," he interrupted her abruptly.

The name was familiar, though in what context Arab couldn't remember. "I'm sorry," she apologised. "I thought Hilary must be your daughter, or—or—"

Mr. Manners came to her rescue with an easy manner that was at odds with his faintly satanic appearance. "Hilary is my niece. My sister is a widow and obliged to earn her own living, which she does reasonably successfully most of the time. At the moment she is working in Ethiopia, so Hilary is staying with me."

"Oh," Arab murmured. "Hilary said her mother is an anthropologist. I thought you didn't approve—" She stopped, looking as embarrassed as she felt. "It was nothing that Hilary said!" she ended positively.

"I think it must have been," Mr. Manners contradicted her. "Unless you've been talking to other members of my family as well?"

Arab went scarlet. "No, of course not!" she protested.

Hilary turned a cartwheel on the dry, sparse lawn. "She says I can go with her tomorrow and watch her work!" she announced.

Her uncle frowned. "It's usual to introduce your

friends when you bring them home," he told her tautly. His eyes flickered over Arab, his expression giving away little of what he was thinking. "Where did my niece find you?"

"She was at Mambrui," Hilary supplied, keeping a watchful eye on her uncle's face. "I met her there and I asked her to bring me home."

For an instant Mr. Manners's face lightened. "Did you show her the pillar tomb there?"

Hilary shook her head, her eyes still on his face. "No, there wasn't time." She sat down hard on the lawn and began to laugh. "I rescued her, as a matter of fact! She might have been *murdered* if I hadn't! She didn't know what to do, did you?" She lapsed into giggles of sheer joy. "She's called Arab and she doesn't know enough to take her shoes off when she goes into a holy place! There was a fight—"

Lucien Manners glared at his niece. "There was a *what*?"

"Was that what was wrong?" Arab put in. "I never thought of that!"

Hilary wriggled her hand into her uncle's. "Imagine being called Arab and not knowing that!" she crowed. "Lucien, did you ever—"

Mr. Manners permitted himself a faint smile of amusement. "No," he agreed gravely. "I never did!"

CHAPTER TWO

"MAY I share the joke?" Arabella demanded, very much on her dignity.

"But it's obvious!" Hilary giggled at her. "Every Arab knows enough to take his shoes off when he goes on holy ground, but you didn't!"

"It's the kind of thing that appeals to her juvenile sense of humour," Mr. Manners added, a smile pulling at the corners of his lips.

Arab bit her lip, her eyes dancing. "Juvenile, Mr. Manners?" Her own laughter overwhelmed her and she giggled happily, unaware that she looked very little older than Hilary in her jeans and cotton shirt.

"You can laugh now," he drawled, "but such an escapade could have had very unpleasant results! The people of Mambrui are the most conservative along the coast, except for the people of Lamu. You could have been in serious trouble."

"I thought I was," Arab admitted, remembering how quickly the fight had begun and her own helplessness in the face of the old man's wrath. "I was stupid, I suppose."

"Very stupid!" he quelled her.

"But I didn't mean any harm—"

"Tell that to them! You're not now in the High Street of your home town, Miss—Miss Arab. If you don't mean any harm, find out about the local customs before you go round upsetting innocent people. This is a peculiarly masculine society," he added with a glint of amusement that was lost on Arab, "which veils its women and expects them to behave themselves. Your *gamin* charm and revealing dress will probably get you into more trouble, not less, as you fondly imagine!"

Arab's eyes fell to her feet. She supposed she had

deserved such strictures, though she didn't like him any the more for delivering them. "Yes, Mr. Manners," she said meekly.

"How old are you, for heaven's sake?"

Her eyes shot up to meet his. "I don't see that that's any business of yours!" she said defiantly.

He sighed, making no attempt to hide his impatience. "You were certainly well named! You look like a street arab in that get-up—"

"You've already referred to my *gamin* charm," she reminded him. "Well, I don't think you're well named at all. I don't feel called upon to tell you what I think of the way you dress and conduct yourself, though I could, quite easily, *especially* when you tell Hilary that girls are more trouble than boys!"

"So they are!"

Arab lifted her chin belligerently. "Not to me, they're not!"

To her surprise he laughed. "I'll bet!" he grinned. "I apologise, Miss Arab, you're older than I thought."

"My name is Arabella Burnett. Only my *friends* call me Arab."

"I see," he said. "Well, Miss Burnett, would you rather have tea inside or out?"

"Inside, Lucien! Let's go inside. I want to show Arab my things and my new dress. She'll know what to do about the hem."

Mr. Manners looked frankly doubtful about Arab's knowledge of such matters, but he allowed himself to be persuaded into the house with a good grace, telling his niece to go into the kitchen and tell the cook that they were ready for their tea.

The house was beautiful. Enormous, brass-studded cedarwood doors guarded the cool, oriental-looking rooms inside. Persian carpets covered the tiled floors, giving a touch of luxury to the plain, whitewashed walls. Intricately carved furniture stood around in formal groups, vying for attention with the soft leather sofas and chairs. But it was the ceilings that brought a gasp from Arab's lips. They were gorgeous! They were as delicately carved as lace, patterned with geometric signs and Islamic symbols, most of them white and clean-looking, but here and there a touch of colour had been added in green, scarlet, or bright blue.

"This house used to belong to the Sultan of Zanzibar," Mr. Manners told her. "I don't think he ever lived here himself. It was falling down when I first saw it, as you can see by the rooms at the back that I haven't bothered about. I'll show you later on, if you're interested?"

"Oh, yes, please!" Arab begged him.

Lucien Manners gave her a sardonic look. "You might like to see the women's quarters. So unlike the home life of our own dear Queen!"

"I thought there was a Sultana," Arab said defensively.

"Oh, there was!" he agreed. "But she was hardly ever lonely, shall we say?" His expression mocked her. "It must have been a rather dull life for them. I told you this is a masculine-orientated society."

Arab sat down quickly on one of the sofas. "You approve of it, though, don't you?" she accused him.

"In some ways," he answered. "I think both sexes are happier when they have a definite role in society."

"Even if the women are bored stiff?"

"I didn't say that," he said seriously. "Women are lucky to have their creativity built in, as it were, so why envy men when they use theirs on the environment and so on?"

"Do I?" Arab asked, considering the point. "Having babies hardly seems a full-time job."

He smiled lazily. "Perhaps not, but it remains the main function of women, even in modern times."

Arab stirred restively. "Do you have to be so patronising about it?" she demanded.

He was startled. "Am I patronising? I didn't mean to be. I was trying to explain why the women had their own quarters in houses like these. Not nearly enough study has been put into the old ruined cities of the East African coast. I expect you've heard of Zimbabwe in Rhodesia? Well we have our own mysteries here as well. Have you ever heard of Gedi?"

She shook her head. It seemed Hilary was right and the only women he was interested in were dead ones. "Should I have done?" she temporised.

"Not unless you're interested in that sort of thing." He paused, his dark face flushing slightly. "I'll take you to Gedi with Hilary next Sunday. It will be good for your education."

Arab opened her eyes wide, tempted to refuse such an off-hand invitation. "Thank you," she said.

He looked at her with distaste, his eyes coming to rest on the frayed bottoms of her trousers. "Hilary needs a few friends," he muttered.

Well, that put her in her place, Arab reflected wryly. Her mouth twitched with amusement as her eyes met his. "It's all right, Mr. Manners, I won't come in my jeans," she reassured him. "I'll wear a skirt just for you, as Hilary tells me that you prefer women to wear—"

"Hilary seems to have told you a great deal in a remarkably short time," he commented.

Arab sensed that for the moment she had the advantage of him. "She did. Everything you say seems to make a great impression on her. I've heard all about your favourite women, and how you're expecting your sister to be murdered in her bed and that it will be no more than she deserves, and how the women won't leave you alone!"

Mr. Manners' expression didn't alter. "All that?"

Arab wished that she had kept quiet. She was saved from having to answer, however, by Hilary's jubilant return from the kitchen. "I've told him to bring *both* cakes, the chocolate one and the other one, so that Arab can have a choice," she announced. "If I bring my dress down now, would you look at the hem?" she went on anxiously. "Lucien says it won't do as it is."

"Yes, of course," Arab said immediately. "Why don't

you put it on so that I can see what needs doing to it?"

"All right," Hilary agreed. "I shan't be a sec. You'll have to talk to Lucien till I get back."

She departed at a run, whistling a tune that had a strong African lilt to it, loud enough for it to be heard throughout the house.

"Do you mind?" Mr. Manners asked Arab.

"Why should I?" she challenged him. "I do know about clothes, you know."

He didn't answer. Arab knew he didn't believe her and she was unexpectedly chagrined to discover that she cared what he thought. The silence between them grew and grew until she thought that if he didn't break it she would have to and she would be bound to say something silly and make things even worse. She sat back on the cool leather sofa and crossed her legs in front of her, fingering one of the earth stains that disfigured the front of her cotton shirt.

"I'm a model," she said, her voice sounding high and strained.

His eyebrows rose, but still he said nothing.

"I model clothes," she added. "So you see, I do know about them!"

His continued silence completely unnerved her. She stood up, agitatedly scratching the back of her leg with the toe of the other. "I'm very good at it!" she claimed.

She read the contemptuous amusement in his eyes and flushed angrily, subsiding back on to the sofa, her ego completely deflated.

"I must look out for you next time I see a copy of *Vogue*," he drawled.

"Oh," she gasped, gnawing at her lower lip. "You might not see me in *Vogue* exactly. I-I do more with the off-the-peg manufacturers."

"I suppose you haven't been at it very long?"

"N-not very," she admitted.

"How old are you?" he asked her again.

She wished that she could put him off with some witty, sophisticated remark that would take the mockery out of his eyes and replace it with something—warmer and kinder.

"I'm twenty," she said. "Very nearly twenty-one."

"A great age!" he teased her. "No wonder Hilary has taken to you. She's all of eleven!"

Arab gave him a dignified look. "There is a difference—"

He cut her off with an explosive laugh. "There doesn't seem to be much to me!"

Arab straightened her back and threaded her fingers together. "Then you can't be very observant," she remarked.

"*Touché*," he murmured, his expression as derisive as ever. "I can see I shall have to watch you carefully."

Tea and Hilary arrived together. The African servant put the tray carefully down on one of the carved tables in front of Arab, turning the handle of the teapot towards her with a gnarled, pink-tipped hand. The cakes he put beside Hilary with a knowing grin at her uncle, turning his black face into a mirror of Louis Armstrong's. His bare feet pattered on the wooden floor and he was gone, shutting the door carefully behind him.

Hilary chose to ignore the tea tray. She pirouetted in front of Arab, looking dolefully down at the very pretty dress she was wearing.

"Do you think it's too long?" she demanded.

Arab went on her knees beside the child, frowning as she concentrated on what she was doing. The hem was too long. She raised it to just above the knee, pinning it neatly, and sat back to have a look. "What do you think of that?"

"It's *much* better!" Hilary exclaimed, pleased. "Could you pin it all round for me? Ayah can put it up for me tonight, but if she can do it wrong, she probably will, so you need to put in a lot of pins."

Arab obediently began to pin up the hem. "I'll do it for you while we have tea," she offered. "I expect Ayah has enough to do without giving her a whole lot of sewing to do."

"Oh, thank you!" Hilary enthused. "There's a needle and cotton in that bag with the pins."

She waited with difficulty while Arab finished pinning and then tore off the dress and climbed back into her jeans and T-shirt, pulling at her uncle's arm and looking hopefully at the cake.

"I suppose you're hungry," he said resignedly. He cut the cake and offered Arab the plate. "Are you really going to sew up the brat's hem for her?" he asked her.

Arab nodded distractedly. She helped herself to a piece of cake, putting it on the floor beside her, and threaded her needle, bending her head over her work.

"You'd better put your cake on the table," Hilary advised. "When the dogs come in, they'll gobble it up down there."

Arab grinned at her and obligingly put her cake up beside Hilary's. "I didn't know you had any dogs," she said.

"Lucien says they aren't real dogs," the child returned knowledgeably. "They belong to my mother. Lucien likes big dogs, but these are only sausage dogs. They're called Jake and Tod."

"They're a living lesson in the advantages of being wholly selfish," her uncle added. "If I dare to turn them out of the best chairs they retaliate by a concentrated session of the fidgets, or by yapping their heads off, until I allow them back up again."

"How odd," said Arab, with gentle malice. "Especially as their names sound masculine."

Mr. Manners leaned forward in his chair. "Could I trouble you to pour the tea?"

Arabella looked up sharply. "Certainly, Mr. Manners. Do you take milk and sugar?"

"No sugar." He accepted his cup and smiled blandly up at her. "I feel I ought to make some such remark as that I'm sweet enough, but you'll probably contradict me if I do."

"Very probably," she agreed.

She went back to her sewing, sitting on the floor with

her back against the sofa, her knees brought up in front of her, to hold the weight of the dress she was altering. She had always been clever with her needle and her fingers flew as she made a series of neat little stitches, turning the cloth at intervals to make sure that they didn't show on the other side. At intervals she sipped at her tea and filled her mouth with cake, impatiently pushing her hair back behind her ears.

Hilary lay flat on her back beside her, amusing herself by looking at her uncle upside down.

"What colour do you think Arab's hair is?" she asked him. "She says it's auburn, but that's red, and it isn't very red, is it?"

"Red enough," he grunted.

"Only in the sun. I think it's more brown, like those polished figures that the Kamba carve."

Lucien made a play of studying Arab's hair, until the colour rose in her cheecks and she pricked herself on her needle.

"It's like dull copper," he said finally. "When the sun is on it, you can see what it would be like burnished—"

"How do you burnish hair?"

"You don't," he said regretfully. "But dull copper is quite enough to add pepper to its owner's temper."

Arab glared at him over her sewing. "I thought dull copper was green," she remarked.

"As green as you are," he agreed promptly.

Arab bent her head lower over her sewing, wondering at the rage that consumed her. She knew he was deliberately baiting her and she resented the fact that she rose so easily to his teasing, when she would have liked to have been dignified and aloof, instead of young and flustered whenever he addressed her.

She had finished about three-quarters of the hem when a light, feminine voice called "*Hodi*" in the hall outside. Lucien Manners leaped to his feet, sweeping open the door, a delighted smile on his face.

"Come in, my dear," he bade the unknown visitor. "I didn't know you were back yet. How's Nairobi?"

"Bearing up with difficulty in your absence," the female voice answered, laughing. "I missed you, Lucien."

"Is that what brought you back?" he drawled.

"If you must know, yes," she said.

She stood in the doorway, her hand halfway up to her hair, to push her curls back into position. But her surprise at seeing Arab there stopped her. She gave Lucien a quick look of enquiry, and then came on into the room.

Arabella rose slowly to her feet, feeling a fool, with Hilary's dress hanging from her fingers, and completely overcome with self-consciousness about her tatty jeans and not very clean shirt. It would have been better if the newcomer had been different. But, despite the hot day, she looked cool and beautifully groomed. Her cool green dress could have been ironed just a few seconds before, and her shoes were so white and clean that they might never have seen any dust. Her hair was elaborately arranged in a series of curls and ringlets that framed her beautifully made-up face. Her features were not naturally beautiful, far from it, for she had indeterminate, flat features and her eyes were pale and rather small, but she certainly made the best of herself with a strong eye-liner and a make-up that made her skin look like matt silk.

Lucien Manners took her by the hand and drew her over to one of the leather chairs.

"I expect it's too late for you to have tea," he said with a gaiety that Arab had not thought him capable of. "Have a drink?"

"Mmm, I will. Something long and cool. Hullo, Hilary, what have you been doing with yourself?"

Hilary squirmed farther away from the girl and closer to Arab. "Nothing," she said.

"Hilary, come and greet me properly! You don't want me to tell your mother that you shouldn't stay with Lucien until you learn to be a nice, good-mannered little girl, do you?"

Hilary looked genuinely frightened. She went forward and kissed the woman on her cheek, her lips trembling.

"Leave her alone, Sandra," Lucien said, taking Hilary's hand in his own and smiling down at his niece. "You can't make children like you. Leave them alone and they come to you."

"If you say so, darling. Hilary is certainly devoted to you." She turned to Arab expectantly. "Aren't you going to introduce me?"

"Miss Burnett, a friend of Hilary's—"

"Of course, dear. *Miss* Burnett?"

"Miss Arabella Burnett. Miss Burnett, this is my sister's sister-in-law, Sandra Dark."

Arab held out her hand to Miss Dark, who rather pointedly ignored it. "Do you make your clothes as you go along?" she asked in light, amused tones.

"It's *my* dress!" Hilary burst out. "Arab is altering it for me."

"I should have thought you were old enough to do your own sewing," Miss Dark smiled. "Did Ruth send it to you?"

"No." Hilary looked decidedly sulky. "Mummy isn't anywhere near any shops. She's in Ethiopia."

"I know that!" Sandra Dark eyed her niece with dislike. "But they must have some shops around—in Addis Ababa, for instance. Don't they, Lucien?"

"Not where Ruth is."

"Oh well, how was I to know? She does such queer things." She shivered. "I wouldn't bury myself amongst a lot of savages without a strong man to protect me. You should have stopped her going, Lucien."

"It's her job," Lucien said, with such superb indifference that Arab was left wondering if he cared at all for his sister.

"She ought to marry again," Sandra Dark opined.

"She'll *never* marry again!" Hilary almost spat at her.

Sandra surveyed the child's furious face and

31

shrugged. "She's certainly handicapped having you hanging round her neck," she murmured.

Hilary subsided on to the floor, looking bereft and lost. Arab gave her a little nudge and asked her quietly to hold the dress for her while she finished off the last few stitches.

"There you are! One dress, altered and ready for the wearing." She hugged Hilary to her. "Thanks for having me to tea, poppet, and for coming to my rescue at Mambrui."

"Are you going?" Hilary asked, near to tears.

"It's getting dark," Arab pointed out. "My friends will worry about me if I don't get back."

"I'll see you out," Lucien offered.

He couldn't get rid of her quickly enough, Arab thought, and she felt sorry for Hilary, whose dislike for her aunt was so obvious, a dislike that equally obviously wasn't shared by Lucien Manners.

She didn't look at him as he walked beside her through the hall and stood waiting quietly as she jumped into the Mini-Moke and backed it with some difficulty around Sandra Dark's scarlet sports car. She swore inwardly at the inconsiderate way the sports car had been left, right across the drive, making it almost impossible for Arab to get out at all. When she had finally succeeded in getting clear, she lifted a hand in salute to Mr. Manners, only to find that he had been joined at the front door by Sandra, whose voice carried clearly through the still, evening air.

"My dear," she said, "do you think she's a suitable friend for Hilary? She looks dreadful!"

Lucien's reply was lost on her, for Arab put her foot down hard on to the accelerator and the Mini-Moke charged down the narrow drive and away through Malindi to her hotel.

Arabella went straight to her room. The bed had been turned down, ready for the night, and the air-conditioning had been turned down in expectation of the cooler night air. Arab turned it back on flat out and the fan as well for good measure. It made a terrific racket, but she didn't mind that. The last thing she wanted was silence in which to think.

She stood in front of the looking glass and took a good look at herself, moving her hair this way and that to see if she looked any better some other way than hanging down her back. Her clothes, she was prepared to admit, were a disgrace. She remembered her mother telling her that shabby clothes were one thing, but there was no excuse not to be *clean*, and she sighed, for her jeans were far from clean and her adventures in Mambrui had done nothing to improve them. Her mother would say that Lucien's reactions to her appearance were all her own fault, and her mother was undoubtedly right, but for some reason, that didn't lessen the hurt that gripped her in the stomach, or her fury at that last parting shot from the expensively-clad Miss Sandra Dark.

A knock at the door was followed immediately by Jill's entry. The other girl flung herself down on the nearest bed, puffing with heat.

"Where've you been, honey? I began to think you really had been carried off!"

Arab frowned at her reflection. "I made friends with someone and they invited me back for tea," she explained.

"Until this hour?"

Arab nodded distractedly. "I'm sorry if you were worried," she said.

Jill smiled comfortably. "I guess I feel a bit responsible for you," she excused herself. "That's what being an old married lady does for one! What are you going to wear down to dinner? They're showing a film in the hotel tonight and I'm told the whole of Malindi will be there."

Arab turned round, her eyes lighting up. "Let's dress up then, Jill, and give them all a show! I'll wear the gold dress and you can wear the scarlet."

"Okay, honey, I'm agreeable. We'd better hurry up, though, if we don't want to skimp dinner. Are you going to shower?"

It didn't take them long to shower and change and it was only a few minutes later when they made their way down the startlingly white outside stairs to the courtyard below. Two Frenchmen, on holiday from their space programme just off the coast, whistled when they saw them and came rapidly over to them.

"We were so bored!" one of them said graphically. "And now you have come to rescue us, no?"

"No," Jill replied.

"*Mais si*," said the other one, glancing down at the wedding ring on Jill's finger. "I too am married, but we can still amuse one another while these two make eyes at each other. My name is Jean-Pierre Dufey, and *mon ami* here is Jacques Bouyer."

Jill smiled slowly, smoothing down her scarlet skirts. "I'm Jill Gleason," she introduced herself. "This is Arabella Burnett."

Arab found herself being warmly embraced by the handsome Jacques and tried not to mind when he linked her arm in his, apparently oblivious of the sweltering heat of the evening. It was hard though to resist his gaiety and when he swept her, laughing, into the dining room, holding her chair for her as she sat down, she felt a swift lightening of mood and began to enjoy herself, putting Lucien's dismissive contempt for her at the back of her mind.

It was not destined to stay there for very long, however. The first course had only just been taken away, and they were waiting for the curry they had ordered to be brought to them, when Jill suddenly nudged Arab's elbow.

"Look at *that*!" she whispered urgently.

Arabella turned, looking over her shoulder to see where Jill was pointing. Coming in through the door of the restaurant came Lucien Manners and Sandra Dark.

The oriental arches with their concealed lighting, highlighted them for an instant before they stepped forward, following the head waiter to their table. Arab had a brief glimpse of Sandra in a cream-coloured silk dress, but it was Lucien who really took her eye. He looked taller than ever in his tight black evening trousers, over which he wore a jade green coat with lapels and piping in a darker green velvet. With his dark good looks, made the more striking by the harshness of his expression, every other man in the room paled into insignificance.

"That's Lucien Manners," Arab told Jill.

Jill was immediately impressed. "*The* Lucien Manners? The one who appears on those highbrow programmes on T.V., telling us all about bygone civilisations? What is he? Not just an archaeologist. I'm sure that's too tame a description!"

"I don't know," Arab confessed.

"And who is that creature with him?" Jill went on, feasting her eyes on the exotic pair as they took their seats.

"Sandra Dark," Arab supplied dryly. "His sister married her brother."

Jill's eyes swivelled round to rest on Arab's face. "You know a great deal about them!" she accused.

Arab made a face at her, aware that both the Frenchmen were looking at her curiously. "The niece was my friend of the afternoon," she confessed. "You'll probably meet her, because she wants to come along and watch us work one day. She's sweet!"

"You say that as though the uncle isn't sweet at all," Jill remarked.

"He isn't," Arab said. She turned her back on the table where Lucien and Sandra were sitting and tried to recapture her earlier pleasure in the evening. "He's the most ill-mannered brute I've ever met!"

Something in Jill's eyes should have warned her, but Arab was remembering exactly how he had looked at her and how he had referred to her *gamin* charms with such contempt.

"He thinks women should have nothing better to do than please men!" she added bitterly. "Any woman who isn't obedient to his every wish, meek and admiring, a—a *sycophant*, in fact, is an object for his masculine derision and scorn—"

"*Miss Burnett*!"

Arab dropped her fork and choked. His hand came down hard on the small of her back, depriving her of all breath. "How dare you?" she gasped. "Creeping up behind me—"

His mocking eyes brought the colour flying into her cheeks. "I wasn't sure it *was* you at first," he said. "Fine feathers make fine birds. Borrowed plumes, Arab?"

"N-not exactly," she muttered. "There are perks with every trade."

"So I see!" He looked her up and down, not troubling to spare her embarrassment as he took in the full effect of the tight gold bodice, the neat waistline, and the long, flaring skirt. "Very nice!" He picked up her napkin which had fallen to the floor and returned it to her knee. "I came over to find out if Hilary and I can watch you work tomorrow morning. Nothing short of a promise to that effect would make her go to bed," he added frankly. "Do you mind?"

Arab shook her head, unable to speak, but Jill had no such difficulty. She looked at Lucien with frankly admiring eyes and said, "We'd be absolutely delighted, Mr. Manners. Come along any time!"

CHAPTER THREE

IT rained in the night. The whole unit waited with bated breath for the magic hour of noon, by which time they would know if there was going to be any breeze or not. Jill elected to go swimming and tried to persuade Arabella to go with her.

"It only means trouble when you go off on your own," she told the younger girl. "Besides, I've been checking up on your new friends and I think someone ought to put you wise to the situation there."

"Tell me now," Arab invited, settling more firmly on her beach lounger beneath one of the thatched toadstool shades that the hotel supplied.

"Well, okay. But I'm not just dishing the dirt for my own amusement, you know that. I've got kind of fond of you, honey, and I don't want to see you hurt—"

"There's not much danger of that!" Arab assured her.

"No? He's the most handsome hunk of manhood I've seen in quite a while, let me tell you! What's the matter with you, if you can't see that?"

"I'm immune!" Arab claimed.

Jill gave her a long, brooding look. "How come?"

Arab shrugged. "I don't like him. He's too obvious himself, and he judges everyone else the same way. I think he deserves Sandra Dark!"

"That's what they say," Jill agreed. "In fact they say he already has her."

Arab felt a tight knot form itself in her middle and was cross that she should feel anything at all. She was being no more than honest when she said she hadn't liked Lucien Manners, and she knew that he hadn't liked her either. Calling her a street arab and telling her off for wearing informal clothes, just as though she were as

37

much his niece as Hilary! And about the same age! Somehow or other, that had been the worst crime of all. Here she was, fully adult, and with one of the most glamorous jobs in the world, and he had made her feel an irresponsible adolescent who had no right to compete with her elders and betters—such as Sandra Dark! Arab's eyes glinted angrily as she thought about the other girl.

"I think you do mind if it makes you look like that!" Jill's voice broke into her thoughts.

"No, I don't! I was just feeling sorry for Hilary having to put up with Sandra Dark. They don't like each other."

Jill's face softened. "I look forward to meeting this young friend of yours," she murmured. "If I'd known how much I would miss my own family I don't think I would have come on this trip! Be thankful you're heart-whole and fancy free, my dear. They talk laughingly of one's spouse being one's better half, but do you know I hadn't realised how true that is! I've left my better half, and more, behind in London. Here we are, with the opportunity of a lifetime, and all this sand and sea, and all I can do is mope for my true love in London."

"And you wouldn't have it any other way!" Arab accused her. She sat up, grinning. "Here comes the wind! That should hurry things along!"

"Yippee!" said Jill.

The unit was being run by a younger man than usual. He was a morose individual, with never a good word for anyone. But he certainly knew his job. He had chosen his models with care, seeing immediately that Arabella and Jill showed each other off to perfection, even if both of them could have been bettered individually. His photographers he cared less about, because he directed most of the shots himself, arranging every detail to his own satisfaction. His name was Sammy Silk.

He greeted the news that the wind had got up with a dubious grunt. "I'm not having a repetition of yesterday's nonsense. If you two are going to wilt away today, I'm looking for another site. There must be somewhere cool in this dump!"

"There is," Arabella nodded, thinking of Lucien Manners' delightful house.

"Where?" Sammy Silk shot at her.

Arab coloured, not best pleased at finding herself the centre of attraction. "I don't really know—that is, it's privately owned, or at least, I think it is. He—he wouldn't like it!"

Everyone stared at her.

"*He?*" Sammy probed, blinking in the hot sunlight.

Jill cast a slanted look at Arab's flushed face and decided to go to her rescue. "Lucien Manners' niece asked Arab back to tea," she smiled. "Hilary is all of eleven years old and, in her uncle's opinion, in need of friends of her own age!"

The shout of laughter that greeted this sally brought a scowl to Arab's face.

"Even Mr. Manners didn't suppose I was *eleven!*" she denied hotly.

Jill looked amused. "But not much older, dear!"

"Anyway," Arab went on, "he lives in a perfectly gorgeous house. You should see it! But I shouldn't think he'd agree to our using it. He—he has decided views about things—"

"A big head?" Sammy put in.

Arab nodded slowly. "Yes," she sighed, "I think that just about sums him up."

"You forgot to say he and Hilary are coming along today to watch you work," Jill drawled. "At Hilary's instigation, of course!"

"I'll have a word with him," Sammy said. "Get going, everyone! You'll be complaining about working in the hottest part of the day if we don't get started. Arab, do something about your hair. The heat makes it look stringy."

"Charming!" Arab acknowledged, making a face at him.

"I'll do it up for you," Jill offered. "Take everything

with you and I'll do it when we get there. I'll come with you in the Mini-Moke."

The two girls set off together, shoving their various appendages into the back of the open vehicle. Arab stopped at the garage for some petrol, jumping out to watch the African as he checked the engine for oil and water and the tyres for air. She found it difficult to make her wants understood, for he spoke only Swahili. Seeing her difficulty, the Indian owner of the garage came out of the office and issued a number of abrupt instructions, smiling appreciatively at Arab as he did so.

"The car is going well?" he asked her.

"Beautifully!"

"That is good, very good. I am happy that it gives you pleasure. I hope you are seeing all our places of interest?"

"We're working right now," Arab told him. "But I went to Mambrui yesterday."

The Indian nodded, his spectacles catching the sun and transmitting little shafts of light across the garage foyer. "I hope you have a pleasant day, yes indeed, a very pleasant day." He patted the Mini-Moke with affection and hurried back into the office.

"How do you do it?" Jill asked as Arab climbed back into the car and started up the engine. "Aren't you going to pay, love?"

"Do what?" Arab demanded. She pulled a couple of twenty-shilling notes out of her pocket and handed them to the African, waiting impatiently for her change.

"Well, honey, Lucien Manners might be the big one who got away, but all the others rise swiftly enough to the bait! Even Sammy is indulgent where you are concerned!"

"I can't say I've noticed it!" Arab grunted.

She pocketed the few coins that the African gave her, without bothering to count them, and drove off quickly down the road. The movement of the car made a wind that blew through their hair and cooled them down.

"I love it here!" Arab exclaimed.

"Despite Lucien Manners?"

Arab chuckled. "Yes, despite him. I hope Hilary comes alone today. I can't imagine Mr. Manners enjoying anything as frivolous as next season's fashions! He'll make superior noises and ruin everything!"

Jill stretched herself elegantly. "I think you're making a great deal too much of this," she observed. "I thought him a fine man and I very much hope he does come. Sammy hopes so too, if only because he wants to use his house, especially if it's all you say it is."

"He won't ask him, will he?" Arab demanded.

"It won't be your fault if he does," Jill pointed out. "Relax' He won't blame the sins of the outfit on you!"

"That's all you know!" Arab retorted gloomily.

Casuarina Point was completely deserted, however. The thatched hotel drowsed in the hot sunshine, a relic of earlier days along the coast, before the package tours and the larger, more impersonal hotels they bring in their wake. A number of chalets had been built here and there, where the guests slept, going into the main building only for their meals and for the benefits of the bar and the shop. Sammy had hired one of these chalets for the girls to change in and Arab drove the Mini-Moke straight up to it, parking it neatly beside the would-be garden that was fighting a losing battle with the coral sand.

Sammy was standing looking moodily out to sea. The notes in his hand fluttered in the breeze, but despite the wind it was still extremely hot.

"I'll take the afternoon dresses first," he told them. "Try the grey one, Arab, and the blue one for you, Jill." He gave Arab a despairing shake of his head. "Try and look as though you have a figure, dearie. Borrow Jill's padded bra if all else fails, will you?"

"I have one of my own," Arab told him with dignity.

"You could have fooled me!" he jeered.

Arab took herself off into the chalet, telling herself that it was the heat that was getting them all down. Sammy had never complained about her shape before.

Besides, it was the dress that was peculiarly well endowed, the others didn't hang round her in folds. It would look better on Jill, so why wasn't she asked to wear it?

The inside of the chalet was extremely hot with that sticky heat that has more to do with humidity than temperature. Arab breathed deeply and sat down on the stool in front of the dressing table.

"I'm beginning to think I'm in the wrong job!" she complained.

Jill didn't answer. She fished a comb out of her capacious bag and began to do Arab's hair for her. With a few deft movements she knotted it into her neck and pinned it firmly in place.

"I don't think you have much to worry about," she said. "That dress is going to look a mess whatever you do." She smiled at Arab's reflection in the glass. "It's unlike Sammy to give you a bad deal like that. He usually reserves the really bad breaks for me!"

Arab looked up, shocked. "Do you really think that?"

"I'm sure of it!" Jill laughed without much gaiety. "I don't mind, honey! I have a big, strong husband to provide for me when it all gets to be too much. You haven't!"

"Nor am I likely to have," Arab wailed. "I wasn't going to tell you, Jill, but you should have seen the way that man looked at me! He told me I looked like a street arab!"

"So you do in those ghastly jeans." Jill looked at her thoughtfully, wondering exactly what had gone on between Arab and Lucien Manners. "I expect he changed his mind when he saw you in that gold number last night!"

But Arab refused to be comforted. She put on the despised grey dress and did her best to fill the bust as Sammy had asked, but whatever she did the line of the bodice refused to look anything but fussy and badly cut. In despair, Arab decided she had done all she could to make the dress look reasonable and turned round to see how Jill looked in the blue.

"You look all right! Very much all right! You'd better try to hide me as much as possible in the final picture."

But Jill shook her head. "Sammy would have something to say about that. Come on, honey, let's get it over!"

They emerged into the sunlight and were immediately enveloped in the business of making the dresses they were wearing look as good as possible in print. Sammy moved them here and there, had them standing with a palm tree behind them, changed his mind and moved them into the shade of an outcrop of rocks.

"Arab, sweetie, it won't do!" one of the photographers groaned at her. "Jill looks great, but that dress does nothing for you."

"Nothing at all!" Sammy agreed. "Come over here, Arab, and we'll start again."

He took her by the hand and drew her across the beach to a palm tree that had been bent by the prevailing wind. Arab did her best to ignore the trickle of perspiration that ran down her back and hoped she looked cooler than she felt.

"Drape yourself over that tree, looking out to sea with a nice, dreamy expression. Lie back, Arab. Hug the tree with your shoulder-blades." He put his hands on her shoulders and pulled her backwards until she thought she would fall and recoiled against him with a protesting murmur. "Look, Arab honey, you're not a shy young girl right now! You're a professional, so behave like one! I'll get this dress to look something if it takes us all day! Now, throw out your chest, duckie, and I'll push some of these folds behind you. Let's have a look at that! Lovely, dear! Lovely! Now hold it!"

Arab sighed a deep breath of relief as the camera shutter clicked and she was allowed to stand up straight and to go back to the chalet to change into the next number. The glare from the white sand and the sea made her screw up her eyes and then, suddenly, there was Hilary dancing in front of her, pumping her arms up and down to attract her attention.

"We've been here *ages*!" she announced. "It's a funny sort of work, isn't it? Lucien says—"

Arab groaned out loud. "Have you, pet?" she interrupted her young friend. "Come along to the chalet and I'll introduce you to everyone."

"Can Lucien come too?"

"No, he can't!" Arab snapped. She pulled at the dress, hating it more than anything she had ever worn. "I have to change, dear," she added.

She ran across the sand with the futile feeling that she couldn't get any hotter no matter what she did. Hilary danced along beside her, asking innumerable questions about what a model did and whether such work could be considered important or merely parasitic, leading foolish women into spending more on badly made clothes than they could afford. Arab thought grimly that she knew where such an argument had originated, and she despised him for it.

So intent was she on her dislike for him that she very nearly ran straight into him. He was exactly as she had remembered him in her mind's eye, his eyes mocking and contemptuous.

"Don't say it!" she almost shouted at him. "I *know* it's a terrible dress! I hate it too! And I don't need you to tell me—"

"Did I say anything?"

"You didn't have to!"

He looked amused. "You shouldn't put ideas into my head. It is indeed a terrible dress! Tell me, Miss Burnett, do you always work as intimately with that pudgy little man?"

"Sammy?" Arabella was astonished for a moment, then her cheeks flamed with embarrassed colour. "How long have you been here?" she demanded.

"Longer than you," he returned. "Hilary believes that it's the early bird that catches the worm. We didn't realise that the morning would be almost over before you started work."

"I must change," Arab muttered, feeling harassed. "And I wish you could think of another metaphor sometimes, other than birds!"

His eyes glinted with laughter. "Complaining again?"

"No, but I'm tired of your references to borrowed plumage and—and being too lazy to get up in the mornings—"

"They suit you, Miss Burnett," he drawled. "A rare, long-legged bird—"

"And I particularly object to being referred to as a bird, even a rare, long-legged one!"

His eyebrows shot upwards. "Was I referring to you?"

Hilary looked from one to the other of them. "I don't understand what you're talking about!" she complained. "Arab, what are you going to wear next? May I come with you and watch you change? Will you show me *everything*?"

"Absolutely everything!" Arab agreed. She met Lucien's eyes in a long, level look. "If your uncle will allow you to waste your time on such a parasitic industry as ours!"

Hilary giggled. "Lucien doesn't care," she said. "It's Aunt Sandra who doesn't think it's proper work. Lucien said she was jealous, because nobody has ever asked her to model anything!"

Lucien's innocent expression mocked them both. Arab blinked, disconcerted by this piece of information. "I thought her clothes beautiful," she managed.

"Oh, very," Lucien agreed. He flicked his niece's excited cheek with his fingers. "Don't be too long," he warned her. "I'm getting bored with the view from the bar and Ayah is expecting you back to lunch."

Hilary made a face. "Can Arab come to lunch? And everyone else? Please, Lucien?"

"If it keeps you out of mischief." He glanced down at his watch. "I shall have to be going in a few minutes," he said to Arab. "Will you bring Hilary home? I'll have to take her with me otherwise. But only if you bring her back yourself, I don't want her cadging lifts from all and sundry. Understand?"

Arab moved her shoulders restively. "Jill and I will bring her home, Mr. Manners," she agreed.

He nodded briefly, casting a meaning look in Sammy's direction. "Good," he said.

Arab held Hilary's hand tightly as they walked away from him, across the dry white sand, towards the chalet. "How long have you been here?" she asked the little girl.

Hilary screwed up her face thoughtfully. "We had breakfast *very* early," she answered. "I didn't want to miss anything, you see."

Arab thought she could see only too well. She had a vivid picture of an excited Hilary nagging her uncle into an expedition he obviously hadn't wanted to make, and her spirits lowered correspondingly. "Didn't your uncle have to work?" she murmured.

"He took the morning off," Hilary told her cheerfully. "It doesn't matter! He can work on his book any time. He said so."

"His book?"

"About the ruined cities on the East Coast," Hilary supplied. "He knows a tremendous amount about them. All about the Chinese, and the Arabs, and the Portuguese, and later on the British. I think there were Persians too, but they're called something else, so I'm not sure."

"Oh!" said Arab, and then again: "*Oh!*"

"Lucien says," Hilary began, "that you're not his idea of a clothes-horse—"

"I don't want to hear what Lucien says!" Arab snapped.

Hilary was not in the least put out. "He says—"

"*Hilary!*"

"But it's interesting, Arab! Truly, it is! He says you were born for better things. What better things, do you suppose?"

46

"Waiting on men like him, I daresay," Arab retorted.

"Would you like that better?" Hilary asked. "I think I should. I *hate* having to change my clothes all the time. I don't think I want to be a model. I shall be an anthropologist like my mother." She hesitated, giving the matter some intense thought. "If Lucien says I may," she added.

Jill came to the door of the chalet, holding out her hands to Hilary. "What have you done with your handsome uncle?" she asked her.

"He's got to go home," Hilary told her. "He has to have lunch with Aunt Sandra. He can never get any work done when she's here," she went on with a remarkably adult air of fatalism. "She has to be taken *everywhere*! I wish she'd go back to Nairobi and leave us in peace, but Lucien says we have to be nice to her because she means well."

"And does she?" Jill enquired, intrigued.

Hilary gave a slow, dramatic shake to her head. "I think she wants to marry him," she said. "Mummy thinks so too. She doesn't like either of us, and I don't like her!"

Jill and Arab exchanged glances. "Yes, well," Arab said, "I don't think we ought to talk about her behind her back, do you?"

Hilary's unblinking stare was turned full on her. "She talked about you," she pointed out, her sense of justice much exercised by this point of morality. "She went on and on about you!"

"Poor Lucien!" said Jill, laughing.

"She did!" Hilary insisted. "She always does! She used to go on and on about Mummy, but I don't pay any attention. Lucien says women always talk too much. He says you have to look for the meaning behind their words because they get carried away by the sound of their own voices!"

Arab made a dash at her small friend, pulling her headlong into the chalet. "*Lucien says*—!" she mocked her.

Hilary grinned, completely unrepentant. "He says you don't talk too much yet because you're no more grown up than I am!"

"So much for you, honey!" Jill chuckled, enjoying Arab's outraged discomfiture. "No wonder he jumped to the conclusion that the gold dress was borrowed!"

Arab began taking off the hated grey dress, allowing it to slip over her hips and on to the floor. "I think," she said loudly, "that if one can't say something pleasant, it's better not to say anything at all! And," she added to Hilary, "you can tell Mr. Lucien Manners that *I* said *that*!"

"All right," Hilary agreed obligingly. "What are you going to wear now? How about this one?" She pulled out the only evening dress of the collection, if it could be called a dress at all, for it consisted of a pair of harem trousers, made of a see-through material and lined in a contrasted colour, and a tunic of the diaphanous cloth, slim and belted. "This one would suit you, Arab."

"How about me?" Jill protested.

But the child shook her head. "I think Arab ought to wear it. It *looks* Arabian!" She searched through the dresses and came up with another one, white and silver and very plainly cut. "You could wear this one," she suggested to Jill. "The jewellery would look silly on Arab, but I think it would look nice on you."

"Very well chosen," Jill congratulated her. "But I think we're doing the swim-wear next."

"Oh, good! Are we going to actually swim?"

Jill crowed with laughter. "I doubt it! In our job, our bathing suits seldom get wet!"

There was a sharp knock at the door. Hilary ran across the room and pulled the door open, her excitement showing clearly in her face.

"Hullo, young 'un," said Sammy. "What are you doing here?"

"I'm visiting Arab," Hilary told him importantly. "Do you want her?"

"Could be. Are you attached to that man who is sitting in the bar at the hotel, by any chance?"

Hilary swelled visibly with pride. "That's my uncle, Lucien Manners!"

"Ah!" said Sammy. "The owner of the house?"

Arab pulled her robe about her and came pattering out of the bathroom where she had taken refuge. "Sammy, I told you, I can't ask him. He wouldn't like it, tripping over our fripperies in his own house! Please don't make him say no!"

Sammy looked at her in surprise. "I don't know what's the matter with you today, Arab. I'm not asking you to ask him. I thought I'd go across and have a talk with him, that's all. I'm calling it a day here anyway, girls. Some sand has got into the camera. For something that looks so pretty, I'd say it was one hell of a pest!"

Arab watched him stomp away across the sand to the hotel. She made a gesture of helplessness. "I wish he wouldn't!" she sighed.

"Why, honey? You make him sound like a recluse! He'll probably enjoy all the fuss of having us about. And if he doesn't like the idea, he only has to say no!"

"I don't think it's fair to ask him!" Arab almost sobbed.

Even Hilary thought Arab's protective attitude towards her uncle a little misjudged. "Lucien will make mincemeat of that man if he doesn't like him!" she announced. "Don't worry, Arab, I'll tell him it wasn't your idea."

That wasn't precisely what Arab wanted, but she began to see that she was in danger of making a complete fool of herself, so she went back into the bathroom and dressed herself in her own clothes as quickly as she could.

"Arab," Hilary said, sitting on the edge of the bath, "did you know that the sea here is a national park? Nobody can kill any of the fishes and you have to have a licence to look at them. There are glass-bottomed boats that one can go in. I'd *love* to go in a glass-bottomed boat, wouldn't you?"

Arab put a dusting of powder on her nose and grinned at Hilary in the glass.

"This afternoon?"

The little girl nodded enthusiastically. "I'll ask Lucien! I'll hurry, in case he's gone to pick up Aunt Sandra, because I'm not allowed to do anything unless I tell him first."

"Not even visit Mambrui?" Jill put in from the doorway.

Hilary chuckled. "No," she admitted, "but Lucien forgot to ask me about that when he saw Arab. He thinks she needs looking after!"

"Well, well," Jill drawled, as Hilary flung herself out of the chalet. "You seem to have made some impression, even if it wasn't the one you wanted!"

"I do, don't I?" Arab agreed with a touch of desperation. "He really is the end! What makes him think that he's such a superior being? I feel sorry for his poor sister! I even feel sorry for Sandra Dark!"

"She was looking reasonably healthy on his treatment of her last night," Jill remarked.

"Only because she's as bad as he is!"

Jill whistled softly. "Honey, are you sure you *dislike* Lucien Manners?" she asked.

Arab tossed her head. "I don't know what you mean!" she said. But she did know, even while she thought Jill was being ridiculous. She certainly didn't like Lucien. Far from it! But he did have a peculiar fascination for her, if only because he scared her stiff! She had never met a man who was so self-centred, so apt to dismiss others, especially herself, as mere adjuncts to his own comfort. No, she was in no danger of liking Lucien Manners. But she couldn't help hoping that she would be around when some woman came along and upset his applecart. That woman might be Sandra Dark, but Arab didn't think so. He would marry Sandra because she wouldn't ruffle his existence, but Arab couldn't help hoping that someone else would come along, charming and elegant, who would knock him and his ideas for six! She couldn't quite imagine such a woman, but she was certain that such a fabulous being must exist and she, Arab, would be rooting for her all the way!

She walked with Jill over to the hotel, wincing away from the heat of the midday sun. She could hear Sammy's voice from a long way off, telling some joke that he had heard the week before in London.

Lucien stood up as the two girls came into the bar. Arab searched his face, trying to find some sign as to whether Sammy had asked him about his house and what his reaction had been. His eyes met hers and he raised his eyebrows a fraction.

"What will you have to drink?" he asked Jill. "Arab, I'm sure, will join Hilary in having lemonade."

Jill smiled. "I'll do the same," she said, amused by Arab's indignant face.

Lucien gave the order and sat down again. "You were saying, Mr. Silk," he said.

Sammy's customary morose expression lifted for a triumphant moment. "Am I a fool then to question my good luck? I shall be thankful to get off this beach, I can tell you, Mr. Manners. If you want the final say in which dresses Arab models, that's okay with me—and with her! I'll just be glad to get myself inside, out of this flaming sun!"

Arab jumped. "Wh—what did you say?" she demanded hoarsely.

Lucien paid for their drinks, glancing at his wristwatch. "I must be off, or Sandra will come gunning for me!"

"But, Lucien, what about the glass-bottomed boat?" Hilary pleaded with him.

Lucien stopped immediately, smiling down at his niece. "If Arab wants to take you, that's all right with

51

me! Perhaps Jill will go with you, to make sure you don't drown each other?"

Jill cast him a flashing smile, such as she usually reserved for her much loved husband. "How kind of you to think of it, Mr. Manners," she said. "I'd love to go with them!"

CHAPTER FOUR

HILARY was delighted when Sammy Silk, Jill, and Arab all agreed to go home with her for lunch

"We'll come back later and go out in the glass-bottomed boat, but I'm hungry now, aren't you?" She looked round the assembled group. "It will be fun having you around all the time!"

Sammy Silk patted her shoulder with a pudgy hand. "We're looking forward to it, sweetheart. We owe you a big debt for getting Arab out of trouble at Mambrui, you know that?"

Hilary preened herself. "You'll *love* Lucien's house!" she said.

Sammy did. Arab watched him uncertainly as he prowled round the ruined rooms at the back of the house. It was the first time she had seen them herself and she was quite overcome by the graceful arches, the flower-covered courtyards, and the crumbling pools where once the ladies of the household had bathed amongst the waterlilies.

"Is it what you wanted?" she asked Sammy.

"You ask me that? Have you no eyes in your head to see what we have here? This is going to be the best work I've ever done, and that's saying something! Arab, duckie, you may not have it all, but you certainly have something! And it's all laid on for us by the great Lucien Manners! You've never worked better, sweetie, believe me! Nice work!"

Arab felt slightly sick. "I didn't do anything," she muttered.

Sammy shrugged his plump shoulders. "Have it your own way! Have everything your own way! What a place! What good fortune!"

"But I didn't!" Arab felt impelled to insist. "I wish you hadn't asked him, Sammy."

"Want to keep him all to yourself, eh? Don't worry, we shan't do anything to cramp your style!"

"I don't even like him," Arab said. "I'm only a friend of Hilary's."

Sammy laughed. His whole body heaved with the effort. Arab couldn't recall that she had ever seen him laugh before, and she turned her eyes away from the spectacle, glad that he didn't laugh more often.

"You're a deep one!" he chided her.

"Don't, Sammy!"

He stopped laughing and looked puzzled instead. "Okay, my sweet, I won't. I'm grateful enough to you for making it possible for us to come here. This is some place!"

Arab was relieved to see him turning back into the morose, rather unhappy man that she thought she knew. He had always been kind to her and he had never said anything out of the way in her presence, though she knew that his language was not always so moderate, and in a way she liked him. She liked him because he didn't worry her, and she didn't want things to change now for no better reason than that she had become friends with Lucien Manners' niece.

"I can't understand why he allowed it!" she exclaimed. "He can't realise what it will be like, having all our gear all over his place for days on end!"

Sammy gave her an odd look. "Don't you? Wake up, Arabella! Or perhaps someone ought to set about waking you up. I think I'd be doing this Lucien fellow a favour at that!"

"I don't understand what you mean!"

Sammy heaved a sigh. "That's what I mean! Don't you know that you're a charming—"

"*Gamin* charm!" Arab interrupted him heavily.

Sammy surveyed her briefly. "I reckon that's quite an apt description at that. Is that what he said to you?"

Arab nodded. "It isn't a compliment." she assured

him. "I looked it up in the dictionary. It means a neglected boy—a street arab!"

"Perhaps that's what he likes about you?"

Arab rejected the suggestion out of hand. "No, he likes his women soignée and sophisticated, like Sandra Dark."

"Did he also tell you that?" Sammy asked.

"He didn't have to," Arab replied. She hesitated, wondering how she had ever begun such a conversation—and with Sammy of all people! "I don't like superior people! *I* don't think he's so marvellous!"

"Don't you, Arab?" Sammy sounded amused, and Arab was afraid that he might laugh again and she looked away hastily in case he did. "I think, maybe, you have some growing up to do."

"I am grown up!" Arab declared.

"Let's see how much." Sammy put his hands on her shoulders and pulled her towards him. Arab winced away from him in a fury, but it was to no avail. He was stronger than she was and he had had the advantage of surprising her. He did not kiss her, though, as she expected. He merely hugged her and let her go. "I'd say you still have some growing to do," he said.

Arab turned on her heel and hurried back into the inhabited part of the house, feeling as though the bottom of her world had dropped out. What was the matter with everyone? *It was all Lucien Manners' fault!* He had begun it all by making her self-conscious, which she had never been in her life before. And he had finished it off by agreeing to the unit using his house, making it necessary for her to see more of him than she would do otherwise. *And*, what was worse, he would probably come along, as if by right, and watch her work, with that contemptuous look in his eyes that made her feel smaller than the smallest insect, and a repulsive insect at that! No wonder he squashed her whenever he opened his mouth!

Jill was lounging in one of the leather chairs in the

sitting room, her mouth slightly open as she studied the carved ceiling.

"You have to admit that the man suits his background!" she said, without bothering to look at Arab. "I'm *flat* with admiration for both of them! I can't wait to tell my better half all about it!"

"Sammy seems pleased," Arab said.

"*Pleased*! Darling, he's ecstatic!" She sat up straight, eyeing Arab's face curiously. "What's the matter, hon?" she asked. "Afraid we'll tread on your toes?"

Arab shook her head. "Of course not! I'm tired of telling everyone that there's nothing to tread on anyway! I just don't like him. Isn't that enough?"

"Could be. I'd say only you and he know that."

"You're as bad as Sammy!" Arab accused her.

"Well, dear, what can you expect? He may treat you like a child—okay, I'll admit that he does treat you like a child. But he seems to be going all out to protect you at the same time." She laughed, pulling down the corners of her mouth in mock envy. "No more grey dresses for you, love!" she teased.

Arab's hands fell to her sides in a dejected gesture. "I can't understand it!" she said. Her eye kindled as she thought about the absent Lucien Manners. "But I'll get to the bottom of it, if it's the last thing I do!"

Jill looked concerned, but then she smiled. "You do that, love! It should make for a really interesting conversation!"

It was difficult for Arab to keep her anger at the boil, though, throughout that afternoon. She had seldom enjoyed herself more. The meal was perfect, with Hilary sitting in her uncle's beautifully-polished carver at the head of the table, playing the part of hostess to perfection. The servants played up to her too, enjoying her small triumph as much as the child did. Even Sammy, who was more at home in an English pub with a half of bitter in one hand, made gallant noises about the food and drink and told Hilary that she had the same poise and charm as her uncle.

Hilary was highly flattered. "Lucien says I'm very like my mother," she told him politely. "He says—" Arab caught her eye and the child choked with laughter. "But he did! He says my mother will approve of Arab—"

"I don't believe you!" Arab said, opening her eyes very wide.

"He did! He did! And I think so too!"

Jill laughed and then she stopped. "Do you tell your uncle what Arab says too?" she asked Hilary.

The child shook her head, looking wary. "No," she said.

Arab grinned at her. "I can breathe again!"

"Why not?" asked Jill.

Hilary took a deep breath, eyeing Arab uneasily. "Because he told me Arab wouldn't like it!" she said with a rush. "But he doesn't mind because he's used to being quoted and he thinks twice before he says anything."

"Does he indeed?" Arab said indignantly. "It's just the sort of conceited thing he would say!"

Hilary, equally enraged, stared at her, two large tears forming in her eyes. "He isn't conceited! He's famous!"

Arab stared back, breathing as hard as if she had been running, but slowly she forced herself to relax. "I know he is, poppet," she conceded. "Jill has seen him on television."

"Have you?" Hilary asked Jill, somewhat mollified.

"Once or twice," Jill agreed.

"There!" said Hilary. "I told you he was famous!"

Sammy refused to go back with them to the National Sea Park. He had other things to do with his time, he told them, rather than look at a whole lot of fish! Hilary immediately began to tell him all about the various corals he would be missing, but Sammy refused abruptly to make any change in his plans.

"If we spent our time sight-seeing, we'd never get through the collection at all!" he grunted. "Someone has to do some work!"

Recognising the signs that Sammy preferred to be left

alone, Arab and Jill neatly sidetracked Hilary into deciding which vehicle she wanted to go in, laughing at her when she decided that she wanted Arab to drive the Mini-Moke because it made more wind.

The glass-bottomed boat was a decided success with them all. A whole new world opened up before them, a world of parrot fishes, dressed in a myriad colours; striped zebra fish; pipe fish with their incredibly long snouts; and the ridiculous puffer fish who blow themselves up like a balloon at the first hint of intruders. They spent a long time watching the parrot fish nibbling at the coral, which was almost as fascinating as the fish themselves. Hilary, who had been taken out goggling in the Park by Lucien, was able to point out the various kinds of coral, the stag's head, the brain, and the potato types, the last one growing in great mounds, amongst which the fish hid and disported themselves.

"Isn't it terrific?" Hilary said, her face shining with excitement.

Arab nodded. "I didn't know there were places in the world like this," she confided. "I can't bear the thought of going home in a couple of weeks!"

Hilary nodded her head wisely. "You've fallen in love with Africa. Lucien said you would. *He* did, when he first came here, and that's why he lives here now. Mummy came first, when she married Daddy. I was born here, so naturally I prefer it."

"Naturally," Jill drawled. "I can see mine is a minority opinion, but personally I can't wait to get back to England!"

Arab chuckled. "That's because you want to get back to your husband!" she accused her.

"Could be," Jill admitted. "But I think I really mean it. I like those changeable days and the bustle of the streets of London—"

"But you haven't got anything like this!" Hilary claimed, horrified.

Jill smiled lazily. "This is holiday stuff!"

Hilary frowned. "But the ruined cities aren't, and

Lucien says they're work. They're his work, at least. He writes about them."

"What ruined cities?" Jill murmured.

"Old Mombasa, bits of Malindi, Lamu, Pate, Siyu, Oja, or Kipini it's called now, and even Kilifi. Lucien writes about them all."

"What about Gedi?" Arab asked.

Hilary tried to look mysterious. "Nobody knows about Gedi," she said. "It's very romantic. You'd better get Lucien to tell you all about it, though, because I don't know very much. Didn't he say he'd take you to see it?"

Arab nodded. "I expect he's forgotten, though," she told herself more than the child.

"He *never* forgets!" Hilary assured her. "And if he has, I'll remind him," she offered handsomely. "He always goes peculiar when Aunt Sandra is around. I don't like her."

Arab felt she ought to protest at this simple statement, but the words died on her lips. She didn't like Sandra Dark either.

"Come on, poppet," she said instead. "We'll take you home."

"There's no we about it!" Jill exclaimed. "You can take me back to the hotel first, thank you very much. I've had enough sea and sun for one day. Besides, I want to write home!"

Arab and Hilary chuckled. "I think you must be in love," Hilary said flatly. "People always want to be on their own when they're in love."

"And how would you know that, honey?" Jill asked her.

Hilary wrinkled her nose in acute distaste. "Aunt Sandra is always telling me to go away and she says *she's* in love. Not that you're as bad as she is!" she added hastily. "She doesn't write letters. She always wants to have Lucien to herself, though, and I like to be with him too."

Jill and Arab exchanged glances. "What about

Lucien?" Jill asked, with a mischievous look at Arab. "Does he want to be alone with Sandra?"

"Sometimes," Hilary admitted reluctantly. "But mostly he says she interferes with his work. He doesn't allow *anyone* to do that, because it's very important."

"I see," said Jill.

The glass-bottomed boat landed them back on the beach and they thanked the man who ran it, Arab pushing a large tip into his vast black hand. He saluted them with a beaming smile, helping each one of them tenderly ashore.

"The little *memsahib* has enjoyed herself?" he teased Hilary. "She would like to go again, yes? The *bwana* will bring her soon! And the other *memsahibs* too!"

"Not me!" Jill disclaimed. "I expect the other *memsahib* will be as eager as Hilary, though!"

The African laughed, his eyes glinting with humour as he looked at Arab.

"Will she come to see the fish, or the *bwana*?" he asked slyly.

Arab's cheeks flamed. She rushed up the beach after Jill, more than a little angry with the other girl.

"I wish you'd shut up implying that I have a yen for Lucien!" she berated her, making sure that Hilary's attention was otherwise involved. "Because I haven't!"

But Jill only laughed. "Are you sure? Not even a tiny one?"

"I don't even *like* him!" Arab protested.

"So you say! It's funny, but I just can't seem to get that fact through my head!"

"You haven't tried!" Arab accused her, angrier than ever.

"Not very hard," Jill admitted. "I'm just wondering why you should mind so much."

"I don't!"

"Then don't try and pick a quarrel with me," Jill advised, still smiling. "It wasn't my joke, honey, so why don't you tell him?" She jerked her head in the direction of the boat. "Okay, I believe you!" she capitulated suddenly. "You don't like him! But why make such a song and dance about it?"

"Because everyone expects me to like him!" Arab sighed. "*And I don't!*"

"So you've said," Jill pointed out. "Only, honey, I don't know why I should think it's my place to advise you—only, well, don't tell him that you don't like him when you're all het up. He might not believe you, and he could make rings round you any time he chose! You may not be as young as he pretends you are, but you're not in the same class as Sandra Dark. It might be as well to remember that!"

Arab was very quiet as she drove Jill back to the hotel. Hilary, however, was pleased to have the back seat all to herself because it meant she could bob back and forth from one side to the other, until Arab told her to sit still, when she subsided sulkily almost on to the floor, ignoring her elders for the rest of the way to the hotel.

When Jill got out and disappeared into the hotel, she climbed into the front seat beside Arab, giving her an uncertain grin.

"I didn't upset your driving, did I?" she said by way of apology.

"No, but it isn't a very safe thing to do," Arab told her. "Supposing the Mini-Moke turned over? You might get badly hurt."

"You might too!" Hilary said, going very white. "I won't do it again."

"That's all right, then," Arab smiled at her.

Hilary scowled thoughtfully. "I wish *you* were my aunt," she announced. "Aunt Sandra never takes me anywhere!"

"Perhaps she likes doing different sorts of things," Arab suggested. "Things that you wouldn't enjoy doing at all."

"She does. She likes shopping," Hilary muttered. "Dull shopping—like looking in shop windows at a whole lot of things nobody could possibly want!"

"I do that too!" Arab said apologetically.

"But not all the time," Hilary argued. "Must we go home already?" she added, stretching her sun-tanned limbs with an almost feline sense of enjoyment of her own physical well-being.

"We ought to," Arab began.

"I want to go to Mambrui again. Lucien says I should have shown you the pillar tomb there. *Please*, Arab, do let's just go there and back, and then go home?"

Arab hesitated for only a second. "Do you think they'll recognise us?" she asked, painfully aware of the outcome of her last visit there.

Hilary looked her up and down, her eyes very serious. "I don't *think* so. Those trousers aren't a bit like the jeans you were wearing the other day. Anyway, they won't do anything to us. It wasn't you they were angry with. They were angry with the boy who took you inside the shrine without telling you to take off your shoes. They know that lots of tourists don't understand these things."

"Are you sure?"

Hilary gulped with laughter. "You're afraid!" she accused her.

"I think I'd feel happier if we had someone with us," Arab confessed. "Oh well, on your head be it—."

"It'll be all right," Hilary confirmed eagerly. "We won't be going right in to Mambrui. The pillar tomb is on the outskirts. It's very interesting. Lucien says that it was still standing at the end of the war, but since then it's fallen down. In a way that's better, because you can go right up to it and look at it."

"Okay, pet, we'll go!"

Having committed herself, Arab was as keen to make the trip as Hilary was. She drove out along the north road and across the river with a feeling of exhilaration that she was going to see something that Lucien thought important. She thought it would be a clue to the people of the coast, who everyone told her were quite different from those of the hinterland. Their long contact with the Arabs, who came sweeping down the coast on the monsoon winds in their *dhows*, had brought more than their Islamic faith with them; they had brought the whole flower of their civilisation, which had sent down firm roots in its new African environment. Other strangers had followed, adding their different flavours to the basic brew, but it had remained true to its first character, with a fierce loyalty to the values that had arrived on the winds as long ago as the eleventh century, at a time when William of Normandy was busy conquering England.

Hilary chatted happily by Arab's side. There were other pillar tombs, she told her. There were two actually in Malindi. But the one at Mambrui was, in Lucien's opinion, the most interesting.

Even broken and lying on its side, the pillar was a thing to wonder at. When it had been upright, it had reached some twenty-seven feet into the sky. Now, the top part had toppled over and lay at the foot of its one-time support. Still intact, in the upper portion of the pillar, were a number of delicate porcelain bowls, half-buried in the muddy concrete substance of which the pillar had been built.

"What are they for?" Arab asked Hilary.

The child shrugged thin shoulders. "I don't know," she admitted. "They're Chinese bowls of the late Ming dynasty," she added. "They're pretty, aren't they?"

"Are you sure?" Arab demanded.

"Of course I am." Hilary wrinkled her nose with displeasure that anyone should cast doubt on her veracity. "Lucien said so!"

Hilary danced into the sitting room ahead of Arab, unperturbed that Lucien and Sandra Dark were sitting closely together on the long leather sofa.

"We went to Mambrui again," she announced. "Arab doesn't believe that those bowls are Chinese. *You* tell her, Lucien."

Arab wished that she hadn't come in. Sandra's lipstick

was smudged and she was almost sure it was because Lucien had been kissing her. A tight knot of dismay grew within her and, if she could have done so, she would have gone out again as quietly as she had come in, and gone away, back to the hotel and the loneliness of her room.

Lucien stood up, his eyes noting the unnatural colour in Arab's cheeks.

"Wasn't it rather brave of you to dare Mambrui again?" he asked her.

She swallowed, hoping to disperse the knot in her stomach, but it refused to go. "Hilary said she didn't think they'd recognise us," she managed.

"And did they?" His eyes mocked her, assessing her cotton bell-bottomed trousers with the same frankness with which he had condemned her frayed jeans.

"No, they didn't," Hilary put in. "We had a super afternoon. I wish you'd been with us!"

"It looks to me as though you've got sunburned," Sandra observed from the sofa. "I hope you don't smart all night, or you won't want to go out with—Arab, isn't it?"

"Arabella Burnett," Arab answered quickly, enunciating very clearly.

Lucien looked amused. "Only her friends are allowed to call her Arab," he explained to Sandra in a deadpan voice.

Sandra was prepared to be tolerant. "These silly names that one's family give one do tend to stick. May I call you Arabella?"

"If you like," Arab said.

Hilary gave her aunt an impatient look and turned back to Lucien. "You tell her!" she commanded him. "She doesn't believe me that those bowls are Chinese of the late Ming dynasty. But they are, aren't they?"

"They are," Lucien agreed.

"I told you so!" Hilary gloated. "I knew they were Chinese!"

"Does it matter?" Sandra asked, looking bored.

Arab longed to put an end to the conversation, but she couldn't think of any way of leaving as soon as she had come. She sat down on the arm of one of the leather chairs, her long legs stuck out in front of her.

"How did they get here?" she asked, pretending an interest in the buckle of her belt that she was far from feeling.

Lucien's face lit with a burning enthusiasm that completely obliterated his former mockery. "They came here long before us Europeans," he said. "There's a fine description of their ships, or junks, in a poem written by Chin Chhu-Fei, in 1178. One can imagine them coming into these ports and selling their wares, just as they're trying to do again today. 'The ships that sail the southern seas and southward are like houses. When their sails are spread they are like great clouds in the sky...'"

Arab's imagination was caught. "Were they as big as that?"

"They must have been pretty big," Lucien answered. "They had a long way to come."

"And they brought the porcelain bowls with them?"

He nodded. "The local people incorporated them into the walls of their houses, probably to keep away evil spirits. They still do in some of the local houses along the coast. Some of the best examples are in Lamu. Lamu bowls, dug out of their ancient houses, are very valuable. One might almost say they're collectors' pieces.'

"Are there any at Gedi?" Hilary asked him, wriggling her body into the limited space between him and Sandra Dark.

"Not the very best examples," he answered.

Arab jumped hastily to her feet before Hilary took it into her head to remind her uncle that he had offered to take them to Gedi the following Sunday.

"I must go back," she stammered. "Jill will be wondering where I've got to."

"She won't have finished her letter," Hilary said flatly. She gave another wriggle, forcing her aunt to give way and to shift farther down the sofa. Arab thought that Sandra could sometimes be forgiven for wanting to slap her young niece. With difficulty, she repressed a smile.

Lucien stood up more slowly, hauling Hilary on to her feet beside him. "Won't you have something to drink before you go?" he asked.

Arab shook her head. "No," she said. "No, thank you." She swallowed. "Please sit down, I can see myself out."

"I wouldn't dream of it," Lucien retorted. "You might steal my best Lamu bowl on your way out!"

Arab started guiltily, bringing on herself another half-mocking smile of amusement from Lucien. She walked ahead of him into the hall, pushing her hair back behind her ears with anxious fingers.

"Do I take it that Hilary was trying to remind me that I'm taking you both to Gedi on Sunday?" his deep voice drawled behind her.

"She—she doesn't understand that you might have other commitments," she said defensively.

He lifted his eyebrows in enquiry. "Have I?"

"I thought—I mean—It doesn't matter," she said finally. "I quite understand."

"It's more than I do," he taunted her.

She could have cried with sheer frustration. "You'll want to have Miss Dark to yourself. You don't have to invite me, Mr. Manners. In fact, I'd rather you didn't, because I have other things to do—"

"Oh?" His voice was bleak and ice cold. "Forgive me, Miss Burnett, but I thought you had already accepted my invitation. Did I misunderstand you?"

Arab blinked, hoping the tears that threatened to afflict her would go away.

"But you'd rather take Miss Dark—"

"Nothing would induce me to take Sandra on a picnic to Gedi," Lucien assured her brutally. "She would be bored stiff as soon as we hit the dirt track. Sandra believes in being comfortable at all times."

Arab blinked again. "Then—then somewhere else?" she suggested.

Lucien's hand closed round her elbow and he steered her with deliberation towards her Mini-Moke.

"Don't be silly, Arab! Sandra and I are quite capable of making our own arrangements without any help from you. If you want to know, she's spending the week-end down at Mombasa with some friends. Now, do you want to go to Gedi on Sunday, or not?"

Arab sniffed and rubbed her face with her free hand. "I think you're *horrid*!" she burst out.

"I daresay," he returned patiently. "Well, Arab?"

"*Yes*! But only because Hilary would be disappointed if we didn't go!" She jumped into the Mini-Moke and glared at him. "I can quite well look after myself, Mr. Manners, whatever you think!"

To her chagrin he only laughed at her. "Perhaps on Sunday I'll find out!" he threatened and, turning on his heel, he went straight back into the house.

CHAPTER FIVE

BUT, before Sunday, there stretched the rest of the week. Arab liked the early mornings best of all. She was woken promptly at seven by the African who cleaned her room, who brought her tea and orange juice and wished her a good day in his country. He told her that he came from up country, but that his wife was one of the local tribeswomen, so he had moved down to the coast. It was very hot, but he liked the work in the hotel. He liked, he said, to watch people enjoy themselves. Arab tried to explain that she was working and not on holiday, but his rather limited English broke down at this point and he hurried off about his duties.

Breakfast was a feast left over from the best of the Colonial era. Arab felt it gave an importance to the day that she had never achieved by grabbing a cup of coffee on her way out of the room she shared with a girl-friend in London. Here, there was a whole table laid out with a choice of cereals and tropical fruits to which one helped oneself, and this in turn was followed by a choice of bacon and eggs, or sausages, or smoked haddock, toast and marmalade, and coffee or tea. It gave one a sense of well-being that surprised Arab. She had not thought that her creature comforts were particularly important to her, and yet here she was, lapping up the luxury of her surroundings just as though she always ate breakfast in style.

The only people who were up when Arab had breakfast were the two young Frenchmen.

"Come dancing tonight with us, Arab?" they begged her. "We'll ask Jill too, to make it all respectable. You come, *oui*?"

"*Oui*," she agreed. "I'd love to. But they don't have dancing here, do they?"

"Not here. At one of the other hotels."

Jacques' warm eyes caressed her. "Will you wear that gold dress for me, little Arab?" he whispered in her ear as he went past her table.

Arab blushed and nodded. "You won't forget to ask Jill, will you?" she asked them, concerned that they might leave the other girl out.

"*Mais non, petite*! We are not as bold and bad as we look!"

Arab finished her breakfast and went outside to walk along the beach before it became too hot. The sky was like an iridescent pearl, waiting for the sea breeze to sweep the trailing clouds away and reveal the royal blue sky and the burning orb of the sun. Then the clouds would cling to the horizon, little cotton-wool balls that constantly changed their shape as they moved towards the high lands of the interior.

From the beach of the hotel one could only just see the wall of Malindi harbour where most of the fishing boats sheltered. The Europeans had brought their own motor-driven launches to make deep-sea fishing safer and quicker, but the natives kept to their own traditional boats. There were the *dhows*, which had first come down from Arabia so many centuries before. These were smaller than those that set out to cross the Indian Ocean and return again on the winds of the monsoons. These were only about twenty to thirty feet in length, with a crew of three to five men, who stay out all day, setting traps for those fish that live on the bottom, such as tafi and lithrenedae. Perhaps the most popular of the local boats was the *hori*, which is little more than a dug-out canoe, mostly imported from Malabar, though they are made of mango wood which is readily available locally. They are used for trolling, with one of the crew attaching the line to his big toe, while the other crew member balances the frail craft in the bucketing waves. On good days they will catch as much as two hundred pounds of fish in the five hours they are out at sea.

The other two craft are not so popular in these days. The *mashua*, the largest of them all, go out shark fishing with nets. Sometimes they are joined by some of the Lamu fleet, who concentrate on snappers. The crews of these boats sleep on board and at night their lights can be seen for miles along the coast. The fourth kind of boat is the *ngalwa*, an outrigger canoe that probably originated in Indonesia and perhaps came to Malindi by way of Madagascar. Their decline has been brought about by their heaviness which makes rowing very hard work when the sails can't be used. They are often hired out by tourists because they look so picturesque. Mostly they are used for catching squid for bait, and then the squid is used for catching the same fish as the *dhows*.

Walking along the beach, Arab could see the fishing fleets at work. She wondered if Lucien ever went fishing and had a breathless vision of his asking her to go with him. Of course it would never happen. She didn't want it to happen! But she would have loved to skim over the tropical waters in such a romantic craft with— She caught herself up with a jerk. *Not* with Lucien! But she would like to go with Jacques perhaps, if he would take her.

She was reluctant to come down to earth and return to the hotel. She had been a model for more than a year now, and she never remembered a time when she had not wanted to hurry off to her work. She had enjoyed it, all of it, from the very first moment. But she knew, as surely as she knew her own name, that she was not going to enjoy working in Lucien's house.

Jill, on the other hand, gave every sign of looking forward to it. She was ready, waiting in the passenger seat of the Mini-Moke, when Arab went to look for her.

"I can't wait to have another look at that super

house," she confided as Arab climbed in beside her. "Someone was telling me that all that carving in the ceilings must have been done by hand. It must have taken simply ages!"

"I suppose so," Arab said.

Jill glanced at her, raised her eyebrows thoughtfully, but she said nothing. "Do you really want to go dancing with those French boys tonight?" she asked instead.

Arab shrugged her shoulders. "It might be fun."

Jill sighed. "Look, love, Jacques has been away from home for a long time. Are you sure you want the same kind of fun?"

Arab started up the engine in silence, backing the Moke out of the covered parking spaces that the hotel provided, and out into the main road.

"Jacques only wants to dance," she said at last. "You make him sound like a lonely wolf!"

"I know," Jill confessed. "I don't know what it is about you, honey, but you don't look as though you know where you're going! I had Jean-Pierre as my partner during the film the other evening, remember? He said Jacques had high hopes of making the most of this leave, even if it meant going down to Mombasa. I think Jean-Pierre was a bit envious because Jacques hadn't a wife to account to for all this experience he hopes to gather. I don't think you're the type to be used as experience. What do you think?"

"I think you're exaggerating," Arab answered. "Jacques isn't the leering type! He never even tried to kiss me, if you must know!"

"I'd be happier if he had," Jill retorted. She frowned at Arab's rebellious expression. "Okay, okay, I'll shut up! If you only didn't look so defenceless and vulnerable, you wouldn't stir them all up, appealing to their protective instincts against everybody else but themselves!"

Arab laughed, "I think you've got me confused with Sandra Dark!"

"My dear child, you must be *joking*! Sandra doesn't

need anyone's protection! She comes armour-plated with her own self-confidence! I don't imagine even a Frenchman on the loose would mistake her for a luscious morsel, waiting for him to gobble her up!"

"Oh, really, Jill!"

"You take the word of an experienced married woman and have a long, cool look at Jacques tonight before you go walking with him in the dark."

"All right, I will," Arab chuckled. "Though if I'd known you were going to take your duties as chaperone so seriously, I might not have insisted that they asked you as well!"

Jill smiled lazily. "Am I supposed to thank you?" she said teasingly. "I like Jean-Pierre, but I can take him or leave him alone, you know. My heart is safely locked up in England!"

"So is his," Arab reminded her. "I heard him telling you all about his wife!"

Jill sobered, looking suddenly sad. "That's what I like about him," she said. "He feels as depleted as I do, and I didn't think anyone could."

"It won't be for much longer," Arab tried to cheer her up. "I expect Sammy will be as keen as anyone to wrap it all up as quickly as possible. He can't expect Mr. Manners to put up with us for ever."

But Sammy hadn't even arrived when they turned into the drive of the Villa Tanit. Arab and Jill stood helplessly in the open doorway of the hall until Lucien's African butler, tall and white-coated, rescued them and took them out into the garden where Lucien was seated, a typewriter on the table in front of him. Arab caught his quick frown at their unexpected appearance and winced.

"I'm sorry—" she began.

"There's no need to apologise. I invited you here, if you remember?"

Arab coloured. "But we're interrupting you," she blurted out.

Lucien looked her straight in the eyes. "I knew you

"Why? We put slavery down!"

"We also transported all those slaves from the West Coast of Africa."

"But so did the Arabs—"

"Look," Lucien pointed out, "it couldn't have been on anything like the same scale. If it had been, where are the minority Negro populations in Arabia, India, or China? They simply aren't there! Yet one can't escape seeing them in America and the West Indies."

Jill struggled with the implications of this piece of information in silence, leaving it to Arab to say, "But there still is slavery in the Middle East!"

Lucien cast her a glance that made her flesh tingle. "True," he drawled. "You'll have to be careful that you're not stolen away some dark night!"

"Who would steal me?" she scoffed.

He watched in silence as the deep colour stained her cheeks. "Someone," he suggested, "who could provide the right setting for a ragamuffin with tarnished copper hair? Perhaps someone with a house like this one?"

"As a friend for Hilary, I suppose!" Arab retorted, hurt.

"Why else?" he murmured.

Why else indeed? Arab couldn't have told him if she had tried. She stirred uneasily, aware that he was still watching her expectantly, waiting for something, though she didn't know what. She fiddled with her fingers and wished that Sammy Silk would come so that they could get on with their work.

"Where is Sammy?" she demanded.

Lucien's derisive gaze met hers. "Making his way to us across the lawn," he said. "If he can ever get past the dogs!"

A brief whistle brought the two dachshunds to heel and a sweating Sammy limped across the coarse grass towards them. "So this is where you've got to!" he exclaimed, easing his damp shirt away from his chest. "Come on, come on! We're all ready for you. You can't stand gossiping here all day!"

75

"I'm ready," Jill declared. "I thought we were waiting for you!"

Sammy rubbed his hands together. "Good, good. They've got the lighting fixed up for the evening wear." His eyes slithered on to Lucien's face and away again. "I—I thought we'd have Arab in the harem trousers and Jill in the white and silver. Okay?"

Lucien nodded briefly. Arab frowned. "What's it got to do with him?" she asked deliberately.

Sammy shrugged his plump shoulders. "Am I running this unit yet?" he demanded. "So, if I want to ask advice, what's that to you?"

Arab raised her chin. "It's nothing to do with Mr. Manners what I wear!"

Sammy glowered at her. "Isn't it enough that we have this fine house at our disposal? Do you have to make difficulties for me?"

"Yes, I think I do. This is a professional matter."

"Then go and get ready!" Sammy ordered her. "What is it with you? Are you thinking to tell me what to do now?"

Arab stood stock still, not quite daring to look at Lucien, but determined to have the matter out in the open once and for all.

"What's to be done with such a one?" Sammy demanded of the heavens.

Lucien put a hand on Arab's shoulder, defying her efforts to shake him off. "Why don't you go and get started?" he suggested politely to Sammy. "Arab and I have something to say to one another."

Arab watched tearfully as Sammy and Jill walked across the lawn and disappeared into the house. She tried to get free of Lucien's grasp, but his fingers closed like a vice about her.

"Now," he said, "what's all this about?"

"You know what it's about!" she sniffed. "You're hurting me!"

He let her go with a suddenness that hurt more than the relentless pressure of his fingers.

"Yes, I know," he admitted. "I'm not at all sure that you do, though. I don't customarily disrupt my working day and allow my house to be turned upside down for *anyone*. Do you understand that?"

She nodded meekly, not daring to say anything at all.

"Nor would I have allowed it this time if it hadn't been for one thing. I don't know how or why, but Hilary is more fond of you than she is of any other female except her mother, so there must be more to you than is immediately apparent! And I don't like to see innocent young women of my acquaintance being pawed by men like Sammy Silk!"

Arab could have laughed, but something in Lucien's expression prevented her. Instead she allowed herself a small, tight smile.

"Sammy is like—like a father to me!" she claimed wildly.

"Don't be ridiculous!"

"I ridiculous? If there's anything ridiculous about this conversation, it's you!" she stormed on.

"Very likely!" Lucien agreed grimly.

"Well then—?" She stole a glance at his angry face and realised bitterly that she was a little afraid of him. "L-Lucien, he doesn't paw me!"

"My dear girl, when you were being photographed in that atrocious grey dress, he couldn't keep his hands off you!"

"But—" she began. She licked her lips and began again. "But—"

"*Yes?*" he prompted her.

"It wasn't like that!" she insisted, but even as she formed the words, a small doubt came into the back of her mind. Perhaps it had been like that. Perhaps that was what Jill had been getting at, not only when she had warned her to be on her guard with Jacques, but when she had said that Lucien might have been the big fish who had got away, but all the others were rising to the bait! "I think that's horrible!" she said out loud.

His eyes quizzed her. "It would be worse if you had no effect at all on the males of your acquaintance!"

"Would it?" Arab said dolefully.

"When you've thought about it," he drawled, "I'm sure you'll come to the same conclusion."

"I'm not! I didn't have much of an effect on you!"

"That, little one, is something you'll never know!" The affectionate amusement in his voice made Arab crosser than ever. *She did know!* She knew exactly! She knew that she had strayed blithely into his life, without a care in the world, and now she would never feel like that again. Now she had to worry about Jacques, and what Sammy was thinking and, worst of all, how she was going to cope with her own knotted emotions every time Lucien came near her.

She made an attempt at a smile. "You told me," she said. "You thought me a street arab with a certain *gamin* charm. A suitable friend for Hilary!"

His laughter mocked her. "For Hilary, yes. For Sammy, no!"

Arab sighed deeply. "Sammy doesn't mean anything."

"Doesn't he? Think again, Arab!"

She remembered how Sammy had almost kissed her in the ruined harem quarters of this very house. But he hadn't kissed her!

"I thought so!" Lucien remarked, watching the expressions as they flickered across her face, first guilt and then surprise, and finally a valiant dignity that told him more than she knew.

"They'll be waiting for me," she said. "Thank you for telling me about Cheng Ho."

She more than half hoped he would think of something to stop her going, but he never even looked at her. He sat down again in front of his typewriter, his notes beside him, obviously glad to get back to his work.

Arab rubbed her shoulder where he had held her, telling herself that the place still hurt though it no longer did. She wanted to know about Cheng Ho and the people of Malindi who had sent ambassadors as far away as Peking so long ago. But she didn't dare to interrupt him again, so she turned and went into the house with dragging feet, and began to change languidly into the harem trouser suit, ignoring Sammy's cries of rage that she was wasting time and that she would have to do better if she wanted to keep her job.

Arab's evening was spoilt before it had begun. The air-conditioning in her room wasn't working properly and she took her gold dress in to Jill's room to change in there. It was only then that she noticed that one of the seams under the arms had begun to come undone and, by the time she had sewn it up, she was already late for dinner and had to hurry to get dressed, which made her hotter than ever.

To her surprise, Jill was already in the dining room when she went to find her, eating at a small table for two with Jean-Pierre.

"I thought Jacques would prefer it," Jean-Pierre explained with Gallic charm. He pointed to his friend at another table. "He is waiting for you over there. Have a good time, no!"

Arab thought it very unlikely, but she managed a smile, and went over to the other table, wishing that Jill and Lucien hadn't combined to make her feel so absurdly self-conscious of this likeable young Frenchman.

"A golden goddess!" Jacques greeted her. "How lucky that I have a tribute for such a beautiful lady!"

Arab hesitated, sitting down as quickly as she could opposite him. "I thought we were all going together," she said.

"We are! But to have you a little time to myself is more romantic, *n'est-ce pas?*"

"I don't feel romantic!" Arab retorted, but he looked so hurt that she immediately regretted her frankness. "I'm sorry," she said. "Sammy made us work all through the heat of the day and then the air-conditioning in my room went wrong. The heat hasn't bothered me before, but today I feel *wilted!*"

He smiled, his warm eyes caressing her. "Yet you look so cool and perfect," he complimented her. "As perfect as my tribute!" He held out a little box to her. "It is a symbol of my devotion!"

She opened the box slowly, relieved to discover that it contained nothing more compromising than the frail bud of a golden rose, still cool from the refrigerator where it had been kept all day.

"May I pin it on?" Jacques asked her, already standing and coming round the table towards her.

She had little choice but to allow him to do so, though she couldn't help comparing his fumbling movements with Lucien's firm, cool hands. *Lucien*! He had haunted her thoughts all day and she heartily wished that his ghost would go away and leave her in peace. She smiled warmly up at Jacques, accepting his light kiss on her cheek.

"Thank you, Jacques. I'm sorry I took my bad temper out on you. I won't any more. In fact, I think I'm going to really *enjoy* every moment of this evening!"

He bent his head and kissed her other cheek in the Gallic manner. "So shall I, *ma belle*, so shall I!"

Arab opened her eyes wide and she chuckled. "You are the first person ever to call me beautiful!" she told him, dismissing the compliment as an enjoyable quirk. "I shan't be able to believe anything you say!"

"But you are beautiful!" he protested. "I find you quite lovely! But, if it annoys you, you can look on it as a pleasant contraction of your name. *Belle, bella, bellissima*!"

Arab blushed. "But nobody calls me Bella." She eyed him dreamily across the table, enjoying his mild flirting. How much nicer it was to be called beautiful than a street arab, she thought.

"*I* shall call you Bella!" Jacques laughed at her. "*Ma belle petite*! Do you mind?"

She blushed again. "No," she assured him, her voice eager. "I rather like it! It's pretty!"

Bella, she tried it over to herself. It sounded older and more sophisticated than Arab. She smiled jauntily at Jacques, wondering why she had allowed herself to be suspicious of his motives in asking her to the dance. "This is fun!" she said.

They rejoined Jill and Jean-Pierre for the short walk down the road to the hotel where the dance was being held. The room was already full of people and, despite the open windows and the fans overhead, the heat met them like a blast from a furnace. Most of the people seemed to be Germans holidaying in Malindi on the package tours that are operated so cheaply from there. A few Britons, most of them air-crew benefiting from the cheap rates they could get for their families from the airlines, stood round the edges of the dancing space, their faces red and shiny from the sun and the heat.

Jacques put his arm round Arab and swept her on to the floor, smiling into her eyes. He was a good dancer, a better one than she was, and he made her feel that together they could attempt anything and get away with it.

"Records are not as good as a band, but after a term on the space project, this is good enough for me!" Jacques breathed.

Arab missed her step. "I suppose you get very lonely out—out there?"

"Very lonely!" he grinned. "But now I am busy forgetting all about that! How could I be lonely with you in my arms?"

Arab swallowed. She found that she preferred to look over his shoulder and to do that she had to stand away from him, despite the pressure of his hand in the small of her back.

"What's the matter, Bella?" he whispered.

"I—I don't know," she admitted. She tried to relax against him, but in doing so, the flash of an orange dress caught her eye and she knew, even without looking, that it belonged to Sandra Dark. She was laughing, too, straight into Lucien's eyes, and he looked as though he were loving every moment of it.

Nothing was the same after that. Arab finished the dance with the now familiar, tight knot of despair in her stomach. When the record came to an end, she tried to look gay and smilingly asked Jacques if she could have something to drink. He went away immediately in search of a long orange squash with buckets of ice in it. Arab pushed her way to the edge of the dancers and sat down on one of the hard wooden chairs that the hotel had provided. She shut her eyes for a moment, closing out the sight of Sandra Dark, who was everything that she was not. When she opened her eyes Lucien was there before her, smiling down at her.

"Don't you feel well?" he asked her.

"Oh yes!" she assured him. "It's only the heat."

"Well enough to dance?"

She couldn't answer him in words, but the heat and the pressure of the people about her dropped away. She stood up and went straight into Lucien's arms, forgetting all about Jacques and the promised orange squash. This was a taste of heaven, to be close to him, to love him even if he didn't love her in return. This was what she had wanted from the beginning of time. *This was Lucien Manners!*

CHAPTER SIX

THE dance came to an end and Arab reluctantly pulled herself free of Lucien's encircling arms. Despite the heat, she felt cold and forsaken away from his touch and longed to rush headlong back into them no matter what anyone thought of her. Instead she stood, with dreamy eyes, pretending that the tune they had been dancing to, of which she hadn't heard a single note, was one of her favourites and always had this effect on her.

"They have lots of the latest records, don't they?" she said, when she couldn't stand the silence between them any longer.

"They do, but that one was old before you were born!" he answered, the familiar mocking expression back in his eyes.

"Oh," she muttered. It was funny, but she hadn't felt at all inadequate all the time they were dancing, but now the tight knot of depression was back with a vengeance and she hadn't the least idea of what to do next.

"Arab—" Lucien began with an urgency she had never heard before in his voice.

"Yes?" She looked up at him eagerly, hoping that he was going to say something that would destroy her nervousness for ever. But he never had the opportunity, for there was Sandra, her beautifully manicured hand on Lucien's jade green coat, smiling at them both.

"Duty done, darling?" she asked him.

Lucien took a quick step away from Arab. "A pleasant duty," he said. He smiled faintly. "Arab dances very well."

"All her generation does," Sandra remarked. "I suppose the coming of the shake, or whatever it's called, has made them less inhibited than we were at that age."

"Are we that old?" Lucien drawled.

Sandra laughed. She managed to laugh without disturbing any of the contours of her face. Arab watched, fascinated, wondering how long it had taken her to practise laughing like that, and thought cattily that it would probably save her any distressing lines later on.

"We aren't children any longer," Sandra reminded him. "I've never thought that children and adults should mix in the same world, have you? It's so unfair on the children. Their heads are easily turned and they think themselves much more important than they really are!" She turned to Arab with a friendly smile. "Present company excepted, of course, I'm sure you are only interested in the delightful French boy who brought you. I have to confess that I drank your orange squash, while you were dancing with Lucien—once it had been suitably pepped up with gin!"

"It doesn't matter," Arab managed.

Sandra laughed again. "I should hope not! Darling, it was only a drink, even if it had been obtained for you by Jacques. He'll get you another, if you ask him nicely!"

"Are you thirsty, Arab?" Lucien asked her. "Seeing I deprived you of your drink, perhaps I should be the one to get you another?"

Sandra frowned. Arab knew that the older girl was keeping a tight rein on her temper and wondered what it was that had angered her. "Leave the child alone!" Sandra snapped. "We've already interrupted her young idyll with Jacques for quite long enough. Darling, I think you've forgotten how much these things matter at that age!"

"Perhaps I have," Lucien agreed tersely.

Arab longed to cry out, No, you haven't! Could he really think that she preferred Jacques' company to his own? She couldn't allow him to think that! But then sanity returned and she realised that he had already practically forgotten her. His eyes were on Sandra and she was smiling up at him, as she had been when Arab had first seen them. Jacques came up to them, putting his arm round Arab's shoulders.

"Will you excuse us, sir," he said to Lucien.

Lucien started. For a brief second his eyes rested on Arab's flushed face. "Thank you for the dance," he said.

Arab swallowed. "You haven't forgotten about Sunday, have you?"

The coldness of his expression hurt her. "I suppose you want me to invite this boy-friend of yours?" he enquired.

She shook her head. "No! He isn't interested in that sort of thing!"

Something of her anxiety seemed to transmit itself to him, for he smiled suddenly, looking pleased with himself. "Then we'll keep Sunday to ourselves," he answered. "Sharing it only with Hilary and Cheng Ho—"

"And the Sultan of Zanzibar!" she agreed.

"Or the old Sultan of Malindi whom Vasco da Gama knew!"

"It sounds too like a schoolroom to me!" Sandra declared. "Come on, Lucien, I want to dance."

Obediently, he put his arm round her, moving with confidence in among the other dancers. Arab watched them go, trying not to look as down as she felt, but in this she was not very successful. Jacques grunted disgustedly by her side, pulling her on to the floor whether she wanted to go or not.

"I thought you didn't like the great Lucien Manners?" he accused her. The pressure of his hand on her back became more gentle. "It won't do you any good," he went on. "Mademoiselle Dark has him where she wants him. You will have to look elsewhere, *petite*, for your *grand amour*. Perhaps you will look in my direction?"

Arab shook her head. "I don't think that sort of thing is much in my line," she told him frankly.

"You think I am offering you an affair, *non*?"

"*Oui*," she said.

"*Mais non*! Naturally this occurred to me when I first

85

saw that you were pretty and unattached. I was determined that this break away from the space project would be the best I had had! But after we had seen the film together, I knew that this was not the right thing for you. With you, I can be very serious—"

Arab stirred restively in his arms. "Oh no, Jacques, please don't! I—I like you, you see, but I could never feel anything else."

"That is because you have not tried! Come, we shall walk back to the hotel along the beach in the moonlight and you will begin to feel the romance of the tropics when you have a handsome man by your side." He danced on in silence for a few minutes. "The great Lucien is not for you, *petite*."

"I know that," Arab said. "As far as he's concerned I'm a ragamuffin, and the perfect friend for his little niece. Not that he means anything to me, because he doesn't! He's far too arrogant and sure of himself for my taste!"

Jacques grinned. "For mine too! Let's forget all about him and his sultry girl-friend. Let's concentrate on ourselves and how much we are enjoying ourselves!"

They danced until nearly midnight. The supply of records gave out and the tunes began to repeat themselves. When they played again the song that Arab had danced with Lucien, she felt she had had enough, and pulled herself away from Jacques, begging him once again to fetch her a drink.

"I think it is time I was taking you home," he said, when she had swallowed down the greater part of her soft drink. "I can lounge the day away tomorrow, but you, I suppose, will have to work again."

"I would like to go home," Arab admitted.

"Then you shall, *ma belle*. Do we go by way of the beach?"

Arab nodded without answering. It might even be fun, she thought. The sea would be as black as ink, and the coral sand would be silver in the moonlight, broken only by the occasional palm tree. The lapping of the sea, and the song of the night birds, would be the only sounds. It would indeed be romantic, just as Jacques had promised her. Romantic and sweet, just as it should be at the end of a successful dance.

They walked together down the path to the beach, admiring the fairy lights that had been placed at strategic intervals to light the way. Arab's gold dress stuck to her ribs and she wished she had had something cooler to wear.

"I'm afraid your rose is dead," she said sadly.

Jacques put his arm around her, pulling her close. "Perhaps we crushed the poor thing when we were dancing. Don't mind, Bella. There will be other roses and other nights to wear them."

"It's too hot for roses," she sighed. "It never even had time to come out properly."

Jacques chuckled. "Then next time I shall give you a passion flower," he teased her. "Will you accept such a token, my golden goddess?"

Arab tore herself away from him, running ahead of him on to the beach. "I don't know what a passion flower looks like," she admitted.

"Exotic!" he murmured mysteriously. "A little like you! Oh, Bella, you go to my head, do you know that?"

"It's the night. Have you ever seen so many stars? I wonder why we see so few in London?"

"Or in Paris. It is the street lights that blot them out. But here they are able to take their proper place in the scheme of romance. It is perfect, don't you think?"

Arab ran farther and faster along the sand. It was quite true that there was a sweet scent on the air that must come from the hotel flowers. Mixed with the ozone of the sea, it was a heady affair, and not one to be played around with. She had been stupid, she thought, to come this way with Jacques. She pressed on as quickly as she could, pausing only to glance over her shoulder and wave him onwards.

Then suddenly he was beside her. His hands came

down on her shoulders and he turned her round to face him.

"Is this a race we are running?" he asked, his teeth white in the moonlight.

"N—no. I want to get home—"

"We are going home. But we have been to a dance together, *ma petite*. Aren't you going to kiss me goodnight before you go?"

She should have known it would come to this! "But Jacques," she pleaded, "it's too hot—"

His arms closed about her, drawing her tightly against him, and his mouth came down on her own. "Come, *ma belle*, give a little! Have you never been asked for a kiss before?"

She gave way to his demands, almost wishing that it did mean something to her, instead of an endless waiting for it to be over. His hands slid up her back, pulling at the tight bodice of her gold dress. There was a ripping noise and she knew that the stitches she had so painfully put into it earlier had given way. With a gesture of annoyance, she pushed him away and examined the damage with her fingers.

"Did you have to be so rough?" she demanded crossly.

"But Bella—" His hands fell to his side. "For you, it was not romantic after all, was it? I did not frighten you?"

"Of course not!" Arab pulled at her dress again. "I've only had this dress a few days. You'd think it would hold together for longer than that! It would have done if you hadn't tried to tear if off my back!"

Jacques stood and stared at her. "You believe, *enfin*— But no, it is incredible!"

Arab had the grace to feel guilty. "No, I don't think! Only I *liked* this dress because—Oh well, never mind why! And the material has rotted and it won't hold the stitches!"

Jacques grinned at her tragic face. "I understand perfectly," he said. "This Lucien admired your dress, and that is a more important event than my kisses, *no*? And to think that I believed you when you told me he was insufferable and not the sort of man you could like!"

Arab strained her eyes in the darkness to see what he was thinking. "You don't mind, do you? It's half true!"

"Perhaps it is a little bit true," he agreed. "It is possible to be afraid of what attracts you. *Mais*, I think there is a little happiness for you there, *ma belle*. He is no boy for you to cut your teeth on! You would be safer with me, even when I tear the dress off your back!"

Aware that he was teasing her, she attempted a laugh, but it broke dangerously towards the end and sounded, even to her own ears, more like a sob of despair. "I don't *like* him!" she insisted.

"No? Are you sure? Are you not a little cross that he does not see you as a woman? Poor little golden goddess! You will need more than a golden dress to compete with Mademoiselle Dark. She is clever, that one! With a few words you are a child in Lucien Manners' eyes! You would do better with me!"

Arab sighed. "Yes, I think I would," she said. "But I *can't*!"

"Then there is nothing more but to take you home to bed!"

The lights were still on in the hotel garden. One or two couples were taking advantage of the warmth of the night to have a last dip in the swimming pool, while an African stood by patiently waiting for them to go to bed. Jacques guided Arab through the bar to the patio beyond.

"Goodnight," he said very gently. "Take a little stardust to bed with you to make sure there are no nightmares." He touched her on the nose with his forefinger. "And no worries, *hein*?"

She reached up and kissed him on the mouth. "Thank you, Jacques. Thank you for taking me to the dance, and thank you for understanding."

He gave her a little push towards the stairs. "*Au*

revoir, mignonne. For us both, tomorrow will be another day!"

She nodded gravely, knowing that he would not invite her to anything again. It was a poignant realisation that saddened her. Was it always going to be the same just because she had known Lucien Manners? She wouldn't believe it! She couldn't believe it! She took a last look at Jacques' sober face and ran hastily up the stairs to bed, fighting with her tears as she struggled with the key in the door. The room was as hot as when she had left it and, pulling off her dress as fast as she could, she threw herself on to the bed and wept the tears of the young and the disillusioned.

By the time Sunday came, Arab had talked herself into a mood of quiet despair. She was sure that Sandra was right when she had described Lucien's dance with her as a matter of duty, just as he had felt it his duty to rescue her from Sammy. If only, she thought, she had not worn those frayed jeans that day when she had gone to Mambrui, he might have gained another impression of her. But what was the use of useless regrets? It would have been worse still if she had never met him and had never heard his stories of the long ago past of the East African coast. That at least she would always have. The story of Cheng Ho would be with her for as long as she lived.

This time she donned shocking pink sailcloth trousers, with wide bell-bottoms that flapped satisfactorily about her ankles. With them she wore a crisp white cotton shirt and a coral necklace she had bought in one of the Indian shops near the harbour. She had some pretty, rather fragile sandals that completed the outfit.

Even Jill thought she looked nice. Her eyebrows shot up meaningly when she came in to breakfast to find Arab already seated at their table.

"You look good enough to eat, honey, you really do!" she drawled as she sat down. "Surely this isn't to impress Jacques, is it?"

Arab shook her head. "I'm going out with Hilary and—and Lucien," she reminded her.

"So you are! How nice for you! At least Lucien will look after you!"

"I don't need looking after!" Arab retorted. "I'm old enough to look after myself!"

"Okay, if you say so. I'm going to spend the day by the pool, counting the hours until we go home. This lotus-eating existence begins to get rather boring after a while."

Arab was shocked by such a programme. "But there are *heaps* of things to do!" she insisted. "I've wanted to go to Gedi for simply *ages*! And you could go down to Mombasa—"

"Spare me that in this heat!" Jill pleaded.

"But it doesn't feel half so hot if you do something!" Arab expostulated.

Jill grinned. "You have a way of making me feel positively middle-aged," she complained. Her eyes met Arab's fleetingly. "Let's hope today is everything you want it to be, hon, and a whole lot more! But leave me in peace to get through the day my own way as best I may. Okay?"

"Okay," Arab agreed. She shrugged her shoulders, laughing. "You're slipping, Jill! Here I am, going out with Lucien for *the whole day*, and you haven't uttered a single dark warning of the horrors that await me!"

"Oh, Hilary will make an adequate chaperone for anyone," Jill returned. "Besides, I have a feeling that Lucien won't allow you to get into any trouble. You'll have your work cut out there if you want to make much of an impression!"

Arab blinked. "You've met Sandra Dark?"

Jill nodded, "That's right, love. Enough said!"

"Hilary doesn't like her," Arab volunteered.

"I shouldn't think many females do," Jill answered. "I can't say I found her very likeable myself, but successful! Even Jean-Pierre was hoping to get a dance with her!" She frowned thoughtfully. "I'm surprised that anyone like Lucien Manners should get caught up in her toils, but I expect she presents a different face to him than she does to lesser fry like ourselves."

Arab helped herself to some more coffee. "I wonder if truly selfish people can make others happy?"

Jill shrugged. "Never thought about it," she said.

They had almost finished eating when Hilary came into the dining room in search of Arab. She came and stood beside Arab's chair, stealing a lump of sugar from the bowl in the centre of the table.

"Lucien is outside in the car," she announced. "He sent me to get you. Haven't you finished breakfast *yet*?"

"It is Sunday," Jill pointed out.

Hilary grinned. "Ayah can't tell one day from another," she said. "At least she *says* she can't! She knows when her day off is, though. The only difference on Sundays is that I have breakfast with Lucien. Usually he's already had his by the time I come downstairs. He says as you get older you tend to have breakfast earlier and earlier!"

He would! Arab surveyed the breakfast table with a feeling of displeasure. It wasn't very late, but she knew that he would see it as another straw in the wind that she was more suited to Hilary's company than his own. She stood up so quickly that she almost knocked her chair over backwards. Hilary rescued it for her, staring at her with surprise.

"Are you cross about something?" she asked her.

Arab forced a smille. "Of course not. Can you wait a minute while I run upstairs and get my bag?"

Hilary nodded. "I'll finish that piece of toast while you're gone—that is, if you don't want it?"

"No, you go ahead."

"Good," said Hillary. "I like cold toast. It's nice and chewy."

In a matter of minutes Arab was ready to go. Rather to her surprise, Hilary put her hand in hers as they walked out of the heavy studded doors of the hotel into the formal, sweet-smelling garden outside. Lucien, in white trousers and a white shirt which set off his dark good looks, got languidly out of the front seat of his estate car and held the door for them to get in.

"Can I sit in the front too?" Hilary asked him.

He shook his head with decision. "It's too hot to all crowd together," he answered.

"I don't mind," Arab put in. It might be a good thing, she thought, to have Hilary as a barrier between them, or at least between her jumpy nerves and the source of her discomfort.

"But I do," Lucien returned. "Hop in, Hilary!"

The child climbed into the back seat, making a face at Arab over her shoulder. "Mummy lets me sit in the front!"

"Which goes to show you have a daft woman for a mother!" Lucien teased her.

Hilary giggled. "It would be a strange thing if I had a daft *man* for a mother!"

"Strange indeed!" Lucien agreed with a smile. "But probably not so daft!" His amused eyes slid on to Arab's face. "Wouldn't you agree?" he mocked her.

Arabella refused to be drawn. "I don't know Mrs. Dark, so how can I say?" she answered gently.

His smile made her tingle with an unnamed and rather frightening emotion. "But you would allow her to sit in the front too, wouldn't you?" he pressed her.

"If she wanted to," Arab agreed. "I don't feel that I have to force my will on everyone around me all the time."

His smile died and was replaced by a fierce frown. "Meaning that I do?"

She opened her eyes wide, looking innocent. "Do you always take remarks personally?" she asked him.

"*Touché*," he muttered. "But if I weren't in such a good humour, you wouldn't escape so easily! As it is, I'll allow you to have the last word—this time!"

"But you haven't!" she pointed out.

He laughed out loud at this sally. "I think you had

the last winning shot!" he told her. "I concede you the point!"

She was inordinately pleased. She couldn't remember that she had ever got the better of him before. Her satisfaction was spoiled though by the knowledge that he was amused by the pleasure she had got from besting him. He might even have allowed her to win, she thought suspiciously. It was just the kind of patronising thing he would do!

"No, I didn't hold back," he said suddenly. "You did it all by yourself, so there's no need to look like that!"

Nettled by his easy reading of her mind, she smiled at him, feeling more at ease than she had with him before. "Was I crowing? I didn't mean to," she said.

"I don't suppose you did. You're a nice child, Arab."

She took a deep breath. "I suppose it would be useless to point out that I'm not a child?" she hazarded.

He looked surprised. "I didn't mean to disparage you," he apologised. "I suppose it's because you're so much younger than either Sandra or Ruth—"

"How old is Sandra?" Arab asked, guiltily aware that Sandra would be furious if she ever heard that Arab had sought to know her age.

"I don't know exactly. She must be about thirty-five. She's a year or two older than my sister, I believe."

Arab digested this in silence. Thirty-five would be the lowest that she would put it at, and that made Sandra older than Lucien. She wrinkled her nose in distaste.

"Are you talking about Aunt Sandra?" Hilary demanded from the back. "She's thirty-eight."

"And how do you know that, young woman?" Lucien asked furiously.

"It's in her passport," Hilary answered. She sensed she was on dangerous ground, for she went on immediately, "I didn't pry, Lucien, I promise you I didn't! She was asking me to admire the photograph she had had taken for her new passport, and it was there!"

Arab giggled, unable to stop herself.

"Well?" Lucien threatened.

"Vanity goes before a fall," she drawled.

"Very witty!" he crushed her. "My God, you're both as bad as one another! I suppose you don't like Sandra either?"

"N-no," she admitted.

"Well, let me tell you, she's a good deal better natured than you are. She doesn't dislike you and she doesn't hold it against Hilary that she needles her at every opportunity—"

"She isn't aware that we exist!" Arab insisted.

"She even suggested that you had more style than I had given you credit for," Lucien went on as if she hadn't spoken. "Why else would anyone employ you as a model?"

"How kind of her!" Arab exclaimed sarcastically.

Lucien glared at her. "It was kind of her," he said. "She knows what she's talking about, as your Mr. Silk would be the first to realise if she had followed her first instincts and had asked him for a job."

"She wouldn't have got one!" Arab exclaimed.

"Think again, Arab! Sandra has had more experience at showing clothes than you've had hot meals!"

"Then what stopped her asking Sammy for a job?" she demanded.

"Your friend Jill, if you must know. Sandra overheard her telling the young Frenchmen at the dance that Mr. Silk had only allowed you to come because another girl fell ill at the last moment—"

"*Jill* said that?" Arab's eyes filled with angry tears. "I don't believe it!"

Lucien gave her an impatient look. "Jill offered to look after you if you came," he went on. "You're very young and inexperienced to be in a strange country on your own. It seems that your employers thought you too young and would be only too glad to have a good excuse to pack you back to home and safety." His impatience gave way to sardonic amusement. "Are you going to cry and prove their point?"

"No," she sniffed. "I never cry!"

He laughed, thereby proving once and for all that he was completely heartless and unbearable.

"Too much of a tomboy?" he teased her.

Arab struggled silently with the lump in her throat. After a few minutes she sniffed again. Lucien silently proffered his handkerchief and she accepted it with dignity, blowing her nose hard and long.

"It isn't that," she said. "It's only that I'm quite a good model and I thought they really wanted me! I photograph nicely, but not so well that I detract from the clothes. It was quite a leg up, getting this job with Sammy."

Lucien took his handkerchief back and pocketed it calmly. "I don't find myself looking at the clothes when you're inside them," he remarked.

Arab gasped and choked. "But—"

He shook his head at her. "Nor Sammy either," he added dryly.

Her cheeks flamed. "But Sandra—I mean Miss Dark—would dominate any picture!"

"I think you make too much of her,' Lucien suggested. "She isn't half as bad, or half as anything else, as you think you know."

"I—isn't she?" Arab said uncertainly.

"No, she is not. She is just a rather lonely woman with too much time on her hands. She would be better off if she had taken up some profession, instead of dabbling in fashion shops in Nairobi, and other such ventures."

Arab stayed very quiet, turning over in her mind the incredible fact that Lucien had actually paid her a compliment. That it had been back-handed, she was prepared to overlook, because she was fairly sure that it would be the only one she would ever get from him. But for a moment it had sounded as though he didn't always see her as a ragamuffin after all. And that was something wonderful to her, it was balm to her bruised spirits.

"I don't mind really that they didn't want me much," she said, sitting back in her seat with a dreamy expression on her face. "It's nice that I came, though. I'd never have heard about Cheng Ho in England!"

Lucien's sidelong glance was as sardonic as ever. "Africa's got you pretty badly, hasn't it?" he said.

She nodded, suddenly tense and aware of that familiar knot of anxiety inside her whenever she talked to him. "I shall hate to go home! I can't bear to think about it! Supposing I never come back?"

He put a hand on hers in her lap, in a sympathetic gesture she never would have expected from him.

"If you want a thing badly enough, it *always* happens!" he said.

CHAPTER SEVEN

"ARAB, don't dawdle!"

"But I want to see everything. Besides, I'm not dawdling! I wish you wouldn't address me as though I were ten years old!"

Lucien's eyes glinted with humour. "All right, my rare, long-legged bird, my little street arab, but may we start to look at the actual site?"

"Oh yes, I suppose so." She glanced at him, veiling her eyes with her long lashes in case he should guess how disturbing she found him. "May I just look at these?"

"It will be more interesting when we've seen the houses that they came out of," Hilary put in, standing on one leg and looking bored. "They aren't *very* interesting, are they?"

Arab smiled at her. "Don't you think so? But look at the porcelain bowl! It's just like the ones we saw in the pillar tomb at Mambrui! And look at these quaint scissors. They must be terribly old. Look at the way the metal has been eaten into by time. I wonder where they were found."

"In the House of the Scissors," Lucien supplied. "Most of the houses are called after something of interest that was found there. The House of the Sunken Court; the House of the Wall; the House of the Iron Lamp; the House of the Venetian Bead; the House of the Ivory Box; the House of the Scissors: those are just a few of them."

"But it must have been a huge place!" Arab exclaimed.

He nodded. "The original town covered an area of some forty-five acres. Not all the houses were built of coral rag, red earth and coral lime. The poorer dwellings would be of mud and wattle, with thatched roofs, and there would be nothing left of them, of course."

Hilary, who had been closely examining the scissors in the case in the little museum, looked up at her uncle with a grin. "Tell her about the mystery of Gedi," she commanded him. "I like to hear about it."

"What mystery?" Arab demanded.

"The mystery," Lucien explained, "is what the town was doing here in the first place. Why was it built here? It's about four miles away from the sea and two miles from Mida creek. All the other Arab towns were built right on the sea, or at least on water of some sort. We know that Gedi was not its original name. That was more likely to have been Kilimani. Gedi means 'precious' in the Galla language, and it was during the Galla advance from Somalia that the town was sacked. That was in the early seventeenth century."

"After the arrival of the Portuguese?"

"That's another mystery," Lucien told her. "The Portuguese never mention Gedi at all. The town was founded in the late thirteenth century, reaching its greatest period in the fifteenth century. It may be that something happened and it was abandoned for a time in the sixteenth century, perhaps it was destroyed by the punitive expedition that was sent against Malindi after they had helped Nuno da Cunha destroy Mombasa in 1529. That would account for it not being mentioned by the Portuguese when they were in Malindi in the second half of that century, because if it was in ruins no one would have paid any attention to it."

Arab frowned. "But a lot of those pieces of porcelain are marked as being late sixteenth century," she objected.

"It must have been re-settled by then, but not for very long, for in the seventeenth century all the Arab-African settlements between the Juba river in Somalia almost down as far as Mombasa were abandoned and left to fall into ruins. Most of them can still be seen, but this is the only one which is kept as a National Monument."

"What happened to the Galla?" Arab asked.

"They fell into decline in the nineteenth century and were attacked by the Masai and Somali. The Arabs from Lamu, under the protection of Zanzibar, re-occupied the coastal strip, which officially belonged to the Sultan of Zanzibar until Independence. The British had some kind of an arrangement with him." He grinned suddenly. "A rather one-sided arrangement," he added dryly.

Arab thought she knew how the old Sultan had felt. Any arrangement one made with Lucien would be one-sided too, and one would find oneself agreeing to it, even *wanting* to agree, for no particular reason except he always sounded so reasonable—just like the British! The idea amused her, and she was smiling when Lucien at last pushed both her and Hilary out of the museum and down the path towards the excavated site of the old city.

The silence was uncanny. Arab found herself listening to it more and more, as they penetrated deeper under the shady trees. No bird sang, no monkey chattered in the trees; it was as if there was no animal life anywhere near the ruined walls of the forgotten town.

"Why is it so quiet?" Hilary asked in a whisper, slipping her hand into Arab's. "I can hear my own footsteps!"

"I don't know, pet," Arab admitted. "Is it always like this?" she added to Lucien.

"Whenever I've been here. It's strange, because it's so beautiful, with the ruined walls and the arches, and the sun glimpsing through the leaves of the trees, and the warm black earth, but the animals don't seem to like it."

"Not even snakes?" Hilary asked anxiously.

"I've never even seen a snake," he confirmed. "Are you frightened?"

"Not frightened," Hilary denied. "Not exactly

frightened, but it is kind of scary, isn't it?" She held Arab's hand more tightly than ever. "I shouldn't like to be here by myself, would you?"

"Not much," Arab agreed.

Lucien laughed. "Beginning to regret your interest in history already?" he teased her.

"Of course not!" she denied. She wished she had enough courage to put her hand in his as easily as Hilary had clung close to her. She cast a swift look at him and found he was watching her closely, his eyes amused. Supposing, she thought in a panic, supposing he could read her thoughts? She looked away with determination, pretending she hadn't noticed the way he had raised his eyebrows enquiringly, nor the way he had allowed his eyes to travel over her, not missing a detail of her appearance.

His smile held nothing but mockery, however, as he held out his hand to her, taking possession of her wrist between his strong, tanned fingers. His touch made her tremble and she concentrated very hard on the path ahead of them.

"Poor Arab," he said.

"Why? Why is she poor?" Hilary chanted, her spirits recovering as they came nearer to the inner wall of the ruins.

"Because she doesn't know what she wants," Lucien answered easily.

"I know what I want!" Hilary said immediately. "I want to go on a picnic every day. Having Arab with us is almost as good as having Mummy, don't you think?"

"Very nearly," Lucien agreed. "Of course she doesn't know as much as Ruth, but she's willing!"

Arab gasped with fury. She wrenched her wrist away from him, rubbing it automatically as if it were bruised. "I'm not in the least bit willing!" she denied.

Hilary chuckled, adding insult to injury. "Not willing to go picnicking with us? But you are, Arab! You know you wanted to come!"

"You'll never get her to admit as much," Lucien drawled.

Arab's brow cleared. "I'm willing to go for a picnic," she muttered cautiously. "I thought—"

Lucien threw her a look of polite enquiry. "Yes?" he prompted her.

Arab blushed. "It doesn't matter." She searched blindly for something, anything that would serve to change the subject. Her eye fell on a large oval tombstone with some writing on it, cut in plaster. "Oh, do look! What's that?" she asked with such obvious relief that Lucien laughed out loud.

"Willing for what?" he tormented her.

She pursed up her mouth with a look that was deliberately provocative. "I'm not willing to be the butt of all your jokes!" She caught the flash in his eyes and retreated into dignity, standing very straight and wishing that she could control the flood of colour that crept up her cheeks. "Wh-what does it say on that tombstone?" she asked him hastily.

"That," he told her, still enjoying her discomfiture, "is the Dated Tomb. Look, you can just read the date here: A.H. 802, the equivalent of A.D. 1399. It's useful because it provides a fixed date from which the other houses can be related."

Arab peered at it, glad to have something else to concentrate on. "Why is it in this position? Are there other tombs here?"

Lucien showed her the Tomb of the Fluted Pillar, going straight on to the Great Mosque, where he picked out the original walls for her to inspect, and gave her a brief idea of what the building had been like. She stood for a long moment beside the *mihrab*, the niche in the prayer room that tells the faithful which way they should face to be looking towards Mecca. It was the best preserved bit of the Mosque and had once been decorated by the now familiar porcelain bowls. Beside it, on the right, stood a pulpit, or *minbar*, of three steps. Hilary climbed the stairs with a suitably devout expression on her face. A minute later she had collapsed into giggles. "At least you don't have to take your shoes off *here*," she said to Arab. "It's just as well. If you cut your feet on that coral rock, it would never heal!" She hesitated. "Would it, Lucien?"

"It would take a very long time," he agreed. "It's tricky stuff."

"There you are!" Hilary exclaimed.

She jumped down the steps and went running off, climbing over the walls of the nearby palace, pausing only to shout to them over her shoulder that they wouldn't be able to keep up with her so she would meet them on the other side. Lucien and Arab followed more slowly, going into the palace through the entrance and wandering from courtyard to courtyard until they finally came to the annexe, where Hilary rejoined them.

"Is this where the women lived?" Hilary asked her uncle.

"I expect so," he said. "Where are you going now?"

Hilary made an expansive gesture with both arms. "About," she answered. "I want to go and look at some of the other things."

Arab watched her as she made her way across the ruins. She felt quite envious of her for her freedom and half thought of following her, rather than being left alone with Lucien. She edged her way out of the palace and walked round the wall, her hands in her pockets, past a pillar tomb, and into a block of houses, where she tried to make out the streets. It was difficult to see what it had been like from ground level, though, so she made her way to one end, climbing up on to one of the walls to see if she could get a better idea from higher up. Lucien came and joined her.

"Are you all right up there?" he asked. "It's a long way down!"

She nodded impatiently. "I can't tell one house from another," she complained.

"I'm in the House of the Cowries."

"Cowries? Aren't they a kind of shell?"

He nodded. "The kind that you can hear the sea in, if you hold them up to your ear—if they're big enough. Some of them are tiny. You're just by the House of the Scissors."

Arab looked down at the house below her, trying to imagine what it had been like. Lucien came close to where she was standing. He glanced up at her, shading his eyes from the sun.

"This house has an interesting well," he began to tell her. "It shared with the House of the Ivory Box over there. It used to be the dangerous type of well, with the top at ground level, making it easy for the person who was drawing up the water to fall into it. Later it was converted and given a parapet—" He broke off, walking towards her. "Come down," he commanded, "and I'll show you."

She thought he was going to reach up and help her down and her breath caught in the back of her throat, making it impossible for her to move in any direction. She took a blind leap at what she hoped was a solid ledge of rock, missed her footing, and fell heavily against Lucien, wrenching her foot as she did so. His arms closed tightly about her and his mouth closed on hers in a long, hard kiss. For a breathless moment she tried to wriggle free, aware of a shooting pain in her ankle, but he held her closer still, his lips moving from her mouth to her cheeks, to her eyes, and back again.

"I've wanted to do that ever since I first saw you!" he murmured in her ear. His hands moved over her, caressing her, until her own arms went round the back of his neck and she was kissing him as hard as he was her. Then suddenly she was free. She sat up, pulling nervously at her crumpled shirt.

"But you can't have done!"

He pulled her back into his arms, more gentle than he had been before. "It was those ridiculous jeans," he told her, then sighed. "It would be easier if you were a little older, my lovely Arab. I feel as though I'm taking advantage of you."

She hid her face against him. "How old do I have to be?"

He touched her face with one finger, marking the line of her jaw and the soft bow of her lips. "Old enough to know your own mind. I feel you're more kissed against than kissing—"

"Oh, Lucien!" she exclaimed.

He kissed her very gently on the lips. "You see," he said, "you're not ready yet to have a hectic affair with me, are you?"

She bit her lip. "Must it be an affair?" she whispered.

"What else, darling? You're going back to England in a few days and I shall still be here. I can't take off until Ruth comes back and reclaims Hilary, and you can't stay here."

"I could come back."

His arms tightened about her, crushing her to him. She met his embrace eagerly, overwhelmed by the strength of the emotion he stirred within her and against which she had no defence. All she knew was that she loved him and that this short interlude might be all she would ever have of him. She had never known such delight, nor been filled by such sadness because it would have to end.

No other man had ever been so close to her and she only gradually became aware of the dangers of her position. She made a soft sound of protest, escaping his searching hands with an effort that cost her dear. Only then did the full extent of the injury to her ankle make itself felt. She tried to stand, but she couldn't. She fell to her knees with a frightened gasp of agony.

"I—I've hurt my ankle," she said piteously.

Immediately he was kneeling beside her, his arm about her waist. "Let me see, darling. Hold on to me!"

She was only too glad to do so. Looking down at him, she could see the way his hair grew out of his scalp, and wondered at herself when her heart turned over merely because she was seeing him from a new angle. How could she go back to England, just as if nothing had happened? How could she live without him?

"I think you've broken something in your ankle," he said at last.

"But I can't have done!"

He stood up, supporting her against him. "Don't look like that, Arab, or I shall have to kiss you again, and we would be much better employed getting you to the hospital."

"You don't understand!" she agonised. "They might put it in plaster! How can I do my job with a great lump of plaster on one foot?"

Lucien's eyes twinkled with silent laughter. "You won't be able to!" he answered with such scant sympathy that she tried to free herself of his restraining arm, uttering a cry of agony as she set her foot to the ground.

Arab burst into tears, sobbing her heart out against his chest. "They'll send me back to England on the first available plane!" she sobbed. "And I'll never see you again!"

"Would that be so bad?" he teased her gently.

Pride forbade her to tell him exactly how awful that would be. "Or Hilary!" she went on quickly. "I *like* it here, you see, and I like your house. It would be dreadful not to be able to finish the collection against that gorgeous background. *Anyone* would look terrific with all that carving—and those ceilings! I thought it was going to put me several rungs up the ladder of success!"

His arms, which had been supporting her in such a satisfactory manner, stiffened and the look of amusement left his face.

"I suppose that is important to you?"

She nodded enthusiastically. How could she say that she didn't care a rap if she never stood in front of a camera again; that she never had cared much, but it had been an escape from a dead-end office job that she had hated. It was only when she had come to Malindi that she had begun to look on her job with new eyes. If it had brought her to such a beautiful place, it was worth everything!

"I see. I didn't know that so much ambition burned in your breast. I took you for a simple girl with simple tastes—"

"Dull, unexciting, and easily flattered!" she finished for him.

His arms fell away from her entirely. She made a desperate effort to gain the support of the wall, letting out a wail of agony as her foot touched the ground.

"Oh, Lucien!" she wailed. "I'm sorry, but you'll have to help me!" She turned to face him, aware that she must look a mess, with coral rag dust in her hair and on her face and the traces of tears still on her cheeks and reddening her eyes. "Please, Lucien!"

"When are you going to be twenty-one, Arab?" he asked in a funny, tight voice.

"In a couple of weeks." What had that to do with anything? she asked herself. She would be back in England by then, just as she and her parents had planned. Her mother had refused to pay any attention to the fact that one came of age at eighteen nowadays. Twenty-one was the traditional age, she had informed her daughter roundly. It was the age when a young man had been considered strong enough to bear the weight of full armour and to take on the responsibilities that had gone with it. It was the age when one had lived in the world long enough to have decided the way one was going to live and not have too many ready-made opinions. Arab sniffed. It was to have been a happy, family party and now—But it was best not to think of now. Now was endless ages without even seeing Lucien. It had been bad enough before, but now, after he had kissed her, he had aroused such a storm of emotion that the mere touch of his hand was enough to set her heart hammering and her knees trembling.

"It isn't very long to wait," he said. "Nothing to look so tragic about."

"No," she agreed.

Lucien sighed and produced his handkerchief again, mopping up her face exactly as though she were the child he thought her. "Blow!" he commanded her. She laughed, taking the handkerchief from him and wiping her face herself.

"T-twenty-one isn't quite the same as being eleven!" she stammered.

He pushed her hair back behind her shoulders and smiled. "I'd noticed," he said. "I think we'd better get you to the hospital, Arab, before anything worse befalls you."

"Nothing worse could!" she mourned. She took another experimental step. "I can't walk at all! What am I going to do?"

"I'll carry you."

She blushed. "You can't. I'm much too heavy for you to—I mean, it's a long way back to the car!"

He grinned. "I have to admit that my kind of work doesn't make one a weight-lifting champion, but I'll manage somehow." He swung her up into his arms and she was immediately afraid that he would find out how badly she wanted to stay in his arms for ever.

"I'm too heavy," she said, her voice shaking.

He set her down on the crumbling wall of the house. "I'm afraid you are for me to carry you that way for very far. I'll have to use what I believe is known as a fireman's lift—"

"I won't do it!" she said flatly.

"Darling, you have no choice." His amusement was very hard to bear, but before she had the chance to object further, he had grasped her firmly round the waist and had thrown her over his shoulder. "Don't wriggle, or I'll drop you!" he warned her.

"I'm not doing *anything*!" she wailed.

He laughed with such a total lack of feeling for her predicament that she took a swipe at him with her closed fist. He responded with a sharp slap on her bottom that brought the tears back into her eyes. "Now will you keep still?" he roared at her.

She scarcely dared to breathe lest she provoke him further. It was a bitterly uncomfortable journey, with the blood rushing into her head. When she shut her eyes it was a little better. At least she could no longer see the rough ground swaying below her. She tried to ease her weight a little, but Lucien's hold prevented her, and after a while she gave up the attempt.

"What about Hilary?" she asked him.

"I'll come back for her when I've put you in the car." To her surprise his voice sounded quite normal. She felt quite indignant that she had so little effect on him. He wasn't even panting!

"Lucien—"

"What is it?"

"I'm sorry to have spoilt everything."

He was silent. He must have been walking quicker than she had thought, for a few seconds later they came out of the trees and into the car park. Lucien pulled open the door of the car and lowered her on to the front seat, keeping one hand behind her knee to support her foot until she could ease it into the space in front of her.

He stood there for such a long moment, looking at her, while she wriggled with embarrassment, uneasily aware that the ready colour was moving like a tidal wave up her face. She refused to meet his eyes, staring down at her fingers as she knotted them together on her knee. He touched her cheek with gentle fingers, turning her face towards him, his lips fastening on hers.

It was a long kiss. She shut her eyes and put her hands up behind his neck, holding him close. The taste of his mouth was ecstasy and she felt cold and weak when he stood up straight again.

"You didn't spoil anything, little one. We'll find an answer somehow."

But she shook her head, determinedly looking the

other way as he turned and left her, going back along the path towards the ruined town in search of Hilary.

Hilary came running back ahead of her uncle. She clambered into the back seat of the car, her eyes dark with concern. "Oh, Arab, how *awful* for you! Lucien says it hurts like anything and that you'll have to have your foot in plaster. We can all write our names on it for you. If Mummy were here, she could do a nice drawing as well. She does beautiful drawings of everything in her letters to me. They're really good, because you can see exactly how the people live, and things like that. Perhaps Lucien would write something in Arabic for you. He could write your name, and his own, and mine as well!"

"I don't know that there's any equivalent of my name in Arabic," Arab said, wincing away from the pain in her foot.

"Arabic is written phonetically," Hilary told her importantly. "Lucien says so. It looks pretty too."

"Hadn't we better wait until she gets the plaster on her foot?" Lucien said firmly, getting into the driving seat.

"But, Lucien, *everybody* writes on their plaster when they break something!"

"She may not have any plaster. She may not have broken anything at all. It might be no more than a bad sprain."

Arab bit her lip. She knew that to be wishful thinking and her misery was complete. If it were a sprain, she could go on with her work, taking off the bandage for the few seconds it took for the camera to capture her image. There was *no* way that a hulking great mass of plaster could be hidden, however, and Sammy would be simply furious!

The hospital was a small building not far from the harbour. Arab had never noticed it previously. She peered out at it, thinking that it looked deserted, when an African in a white, flapping coat came out to the car.

"*Jambo, bwana. Habari?*"

Lucien responded in kind and then went on to tell him about Arab's ankle. "Is the doctor here?"

The African shook his head. "It is Sunday," he answered.

"We'll come inside," Lucien decided, taking command with all his usual arrogance and self-confidence. "I'll give the doctor a ring from there."

The African brought out a wheel-chair that must have been left behind by some patient from a previous century. He grinned happily at Arab, patting the seat invitingly. Arab made a movement towards getting out of the car, but she was saved from having to put her foot to the ground by Lucien lifting her bodily out, placing her gently in the waiting chair. His gentleness made her want to cry again. She bit her lip harder than ever. Whatever was the matter with her, crying at the slightest thing, when she *never cried*! She *despised* people who wept all over people! She despised herself for the unaccountable weakness that engulfed her.

The inside of the hospital was fresh and clean. The African wheeled her in to the surgery, drawing the chair up in front of the window so that she could look out at the flowering shrubs outside. When he went out, he left the door open, and went and stood beside Lucien, anxious to help him as he telephoned for the doctor. Arab listened to the conversation, but she could understand very little of it, for most of it seemed to be in Swahili.

She turned her head and saw Hilary standing nervously outside.

"Come in and talk to me," she suggested to her.

Hilary came up beside her, lounging against the open window. "I don't like the smell," she complained.

"It's only disinfectant," Arab told her.

Hilary went on twitching her nostrils. Arab wondered if she ought to send the child back to the car, but she didn't like to interfere when Lucien was there and well able to look after his own niece.

"Can you understand what they're saying?" she asked the child, determined to divert her attention.

Hilary nodded. "The doctor's coming now," she answered. "He came from Europe somewhere before the war. His English is funny."

His English was decidedly odd. He was a small, round man, with very little hair and a lot of gold in his teeth. But he was kind and his hands, as they examined her ankle, were very gentle.

"It is break!" he announced, and smiled reassuringly round the room. "There is displaced bone. Necessary put right. Then plaster. I do it now."

Lucien's dark eyes met Arab's. "Are you ready?" he asked her.

She swallowed. "Will you hold my hand?" she asked him, not caring if he thought her silly at that particular moment.

"*I'll* hold your hand!" Hilary offered. "And I'll talk to you all the time." She put her hand quickly in Arab's, her face quite as pale and wan as the patient's. "Lucien can hold your other hand," she added in a strangled voice.

The ordeal was over in a matter of minutes. A single wave of pain travelled up Arab's leg, bringing a gasp to her lips. It subsided into a dull ache and she felt able to breathe again. It wasn't Hilary who talked to her, though, it was Lucien. He spoke from a great distance and she couldn't concentrate on what he was saying, which confused her.

"You'd better come home with us," he said. "Ayah can look after you."

"But I can't!" she protested.

His eyes laughed at her. "I'm hardly going to seduce you, my love, while you've got that on your foot. Anyway, Sandra will be back later on. So do you think you could do as you're told without a long argument?"

It wouldn't do, of course, she told herself over and

over again. But she was too tired to do anything about it. She felt funny in the head and she was scared that he would leave her alone at the hospital, unable to make herself understood by anyone, if she made a fuss.

"Yes, Lucien." Her ears were singing and she felt terribly hot. And then she began to shiver and, once she had started, she couldn't stop. "I'd like that," she said.

CHAPTER EIGHT

HILARY sat on the end of the bed, swinging her legs to and fro as she thoughtfully regarded the occupant. Arab pulled herself farther up the bed and frowned.

"I feel awful!" she announced.

"You look awful," Hilary told her. "One always does with malaria. Lucien says you ought to know better at your age than to open the netting windows of your room. It couldn't make anything any cooler. And why weren't you taking paludrin?"

Arab looked suitably chastened. "I forgot," she admitted. "And I don't mind saying that if the air-conditioning broke down in Lucien's room, I bet he'd open everything he could too!"

"Lucien says you think in a typically female way. In fact that you hardly think at all!"

Arab gave her a sulky look. "I don't want to hear what Lucien says!"

Hilary grinned, rolling her eyes with unwonted drama. "He was simply *furious*," she giggled. "Ayah actually *ran* when she was getting your room ready!"

Arab's head fell back against her pillows. The singing in her ears was back again and her head ached. "Must you swing your legs like that?" she complained.

"Sorry," said Hilary. She pushed herself farther on to the bed with a magnificent disregard for Arab's broken ankle. "Lucien says," she went on happily, "that you probably had fever deliberately so that you wouldn't have to go home. Did you, Arab? I mean, you could hardly have enticed a tame mosquito into your room, could you?"

"Certainly not!" Arab said shortly.

"That's what I thought," Hilary said, glad to have her opinion confirmed. "I think he was joking. He looked—well, you know how he looks when he's got the better of one."

Arab did indeed. "Has Sammy been?" she asked.

Hilary shook her head. "But you don't have to worry, Arab. Lucien says he'll attend to him. You have to concentrate on getting better."

The tears slipped easily between Arab's eyelids. Oh no, she thought, I can't be crying again! She sniffed, searching for a handkerchief, but there was none. This was awful, she thought. She sniffed again, aware of Hilary's patient sigh and feeling thoroughly shamed by her own weakness.

"I can't leave everything to Lucien!" she exclaimed, wildly tossing the pillows about in a more determined search for a handkerchief.

Hilary uttered a startled gasp and Arab became aware of a handkerchief being held out to her. She snatched at it and blew her nose violently, making her head ache worse than ever.

"What can't you leave to me?" Lucien asked her.

She raised defiant eyes. "I feel awful!" she wailed. "And don't tell me I look awful, because Hilary has already told me that! And don't tell me that it's all my own fault, because that message has already been relayed to me as well!"

Hilary had the grace to look ashamed. "I didn't say it was *actually* your own fault. I said Lucien had said you ought to know better—"

Lucien looked down at his niece. "This is the time for you to make a graceful exit," he told her.

"No!" Arab exclaimed. "Hilary, don't go!" But she was too late; the little girl, taking one look at her uncle's determined expression, had already gone.

Arab pulled the sheet up to her chin and wished that Lucien would go too. She didn't have to look at him to see the mocking expression on his face. She clutched his handkerchief in a little ball in one fist, hoping vainly that her moment of tears was over.

"I want to go back to the hotel!"

"Having made such a bird's nest of your bed, I'm not surprised," Lucien observed.

"I was looking for a handkerchief."

He smiled. "Don't you ever have one?"

"S-sometimes." She settled the sheet more firmly about her. "Paper handkerchiefs are much more hygienic."

"Undoubtedly. Shall I get Jill to buy you some when she brings your things over?"

Arab closed her eyes. "Jill can't drive," she said. She opened her eyes again, peering up at him cautiously. "Whose nightie have I got on? Sandra's?"

"Sandra's would be a bit on the big side for you," he drawled. "That one belongs to Ruth. Any objections?"

"No." She blushed. "Is Sandra back from Mombasa?"

"I expect so. Do you want her to come and see you?"

Arab shook her head. "I—I didn't hear her arrive," she muttered. "I expected to, because I can hear everyone else coming up and down the stairs."

"Arabella Burnett!" he mocked her. "Contrary to any illusions you may have of me, Sandra does not live with me, in any sense of the word!"

"Oh." Her ears buzzed madly. "I thought she was staying with you," she tried to explain. "After all, she is a kind of relation, isn't she?"

"No, she is not."

"But she is!" Arab objected perversely. "She's your sister's sister-in-law."

Lucien grunted. "Hardly close enough for us to live under the same roof and expect to get away with it! Malindi is a hotbed of gossip, and Sandra is too nice a person not to care what's said about her."

Arab digested this in silence. She came to the conclusion that she didn't agree with him. Sandra, she thought, would be happy to be talked about if her name were being linked with Lucien's, especially if it were to lead to a closer relationship. Then another thought struck her. Her eyes widened and she stared up at him.

"But *I'm* staying here!"

"So you are!"

"But—but, Lucien—"

His laughter disconcerted her. "Shall I fix your pillows for you?" he offered solicitously.

"No! I want to go back to the hotel. Besides," she added, "I like my pillows this way!"

He sat down on the edge of the bed. "How's the ankle?" he asked in quite different, almost businesslike tones.

"It aches, but it's not too bad." She wished the buzzing in her ears would stop. If she felt better, it would be easier to make up her mind what to do, instead of getting in a dither. *She had to go back to the hotel!* "I'm awfully sorry," she said aloud, "but I'm afraid I'm going to be sick!"

Lucien was galvanised into action. "Ayah!" he roared. Arab gulped helplessly. "*Ayah!*" he shouted again.

The African woman waddled into the room, grasping her bulky frame somewhere round her middle. When she saw Arab's face, she bowed her head with laughter, putting her hands up to hide her broad smile.

"That man not going to hurt you," she said soothingly. "Come on, Ayah is here. Little while and you feel better! I put this bed to rights and then you sleep." She frowned at Lucien. "Can't you see that girl is sick?" she demanded. "Why you come in here and frighten her?"

Lucien eyed Arab's face suspiciously. "*I* frighten *her*?" he exclaimed. "Don't you believe it! She's not frightened of me. She's frightened of herself and—"

"Go away!" Arab moaned.

He bent down and kissed her softly on the lips "Believe me," he said, "when I want to frighten you, you'll stay frightened! But you have nothing to be afraid of—at the moment. So you can stop looking like a half-hatched chick and pretty yourself up to receive the doctor. If you want *me*, you can send for me, otherwise I'll wait until you feel more yourself. All right?"

"No, it's not all right! I can't stay here! I want to go back to the hotel!"

This final effort was almost too much for Arab. She thought perhaps she really was going to be sick. Her whole body ached and itched with sweat, and yet she was cold and she was starting to shiver again.

"Lucien," she whispered, "please don't go yet. It's coming back again and I don't know what to do!"

He uttered a series of abrupt commands to Ayah, while he himself raised her in the bed, pulling her pillows into place. "Poor little street arab," he said in a voice so full of amused affection that she was afraid she was going to cry again.

"I don't know what's the matter with me!" she berated herself.

"Don't you? Darling, I wish you wouldn't worry yourself now. Isn't a dose of malaria and a broken ankle enough to be going on with?"

"But I don't want to be a nuisance to you—Sandra might not understand that—that I'm ill. Nor will Jill. She doesn't think I have any sense at all!"

"Nor have you!" He put a finger across her mouth to prevent her retort. "Jill is very fond of you and I won't hear a word against her. As a matter of fact, she's downstairs now. Shall I ask her to stay the night?"

Arab's face cleared as if by magic. "Oh yes!" she exclaimed. "Would you mind, Lucien? It would make everything all right!"

"*Everything?*" The sardonic expression in his eyes confused her. She began to shiver in earnest and she clenched her teeth together. His concern for her was warming and a wave of weariness swept over her as she tried to concentrate on what he was saying to her. Something about Ayah changing her nightie and her sheets and making her more comfortable. But she didn't seriously expect to be comfortable ever again. The prickling heat down her back and under her arms made her fractious, and her ankle ached.

Then, almost before she was aware, she was magically

back betwen dry sheets and her hot pillows were cool and fresh. With a sigh of content, she turned over on her side and slept.

When she woke, the fever had gone away and she was pleasantly cool all over. She was also very weak, as she discovered when she tried to ease herself against her pillows. It was only then that she became aware of Sandra Dark sitting in the easy chair facing her.

"Have—have you been here long?" she asked in a polite voice.

"It's seemed like days, but in actual fact I guess it's only a couple of hours," Sandra answered. "I thought you were never going to wake up!"

"I'm sorry," Arab said.

Sandra shrugged. "Why? You could probably do with it. Lucien said you were feeling lousy last night—"

"Last night?"

Sandra laughed, managing not to crease her face despite what seemed to be genuine amusement. "That's right! This is Monday morning." She admired her immaculately enamelled nails without looking at Arab. "That's what I'm doing here," she said.

Arab blinked. She watched the older woman cautiously, wondering what it was that she wanted. Sandra glanced up from her nails and smiled briefly.

"I'm not going to pretend that I like asking you this," she went on. "I don't. But you seem to have a way with you as far as the people you work with are concerned. Sammy would just love to use me, but for some reason he seemed to think you ought to be consulted, or something."

"I see," said Arab.

"I thought you might. Though it can't matter to you either way! I want your job, Miss Burnett, and I intend to have it!"

Arab fiddled idly with the edge of her sheet. "Oh?" she murmured.

"It's just what I need at this moment. I threw up my

job in Nairobi. It was quite impossible to get anyone to see sense about anything there. One would think that there weren't any Europeans left to buy any clothes, to hear them talk! And do you see me selling anything but what might be a Paris model, if you didn't look too closely, of course?"

Arab looked at her visitor with a certain amusement. "These are not Paris models, Miss Dark. They're strictly off-the-peg models for the mass market. Sammy does the brochures for them and it was he who thought a glamorous background would be a good selling point. The magazines use them, so why not us?"

Sandra lent forward in her chair, her eyes shining. "But Sammy does other stuff—I've looked him up. This would only be the beginning!"

"A lot of models have thought the same!" Arab warned her.

"Including you?"

"Including me," Arab admitted. "I don't aspire to the heights of the profession, or anything like that, but I want to do a bit better than I have so far. I thought Sammy would help me do that. I didn't know then that I was only filling in for someone else."

"That's what he told me," Sandra agreed. Her eyes narrowed thoughtfully. "Now I'm not so sure. He was in quite a way when he heard about your ankle. It made me wonder if you weren't more important to him than I'd thought."

The enquiry in her voice made Arab wince. "Nobody is important to Sammy," she said.

"My dear," Sandra drawled, "he's a man, isn't he? Or didn't it occur to you to play that particular trump?"

Arab flushed with embarrassment. "I—I—" she stammered.

"Oh, come on! You're not so backward when it comes to Lucien!" Sandra exclaimed. "I suppose you think it's different because you're in love with him! Well, I don't mind admitting that I'm in love with him too, and can have him any time I choose, but that won't stop me

120

stringing Sammy along." She laughed softly. "Have I shocked you? How deliciously young you are, my dear! But it puts you at rather a disadvantage as far as Lucien is concerned, doesn't it? I'm afraid he'll always see you as Hilary's little friend!"

"I don't think that's any business of yours!" Arab declared. She longed to escape from this whole distasteful conversation, but there was no way out. She was tethered to her bed by her ankle and the weakness that was the aftermath of fever. She had never realised before how very vulnerable one was in bed in the face of an unwelcome visitor and she cast Sandra a resentful look, wondering if she could tell her that she wanted to visit the bathroom and would need Ayah's help to get there.

"Oh, I think it is," Sandra contradicted, looking amused. "*All* Lucien's reactions are my business, my dear. The Darks and the Manners are meant for each other! Ruth and my brother, me and Lucien—it's always been like that!"

Arab tried to think of some way to turn the conversation. "How did your brother die?" she asked.

"Unnecessarily," Sandra returned. "He went up to the Northern Frontier to investigate some incident and was killed in a border skirmish. He didn't have to go! It wasn't as though it was his responsibility! If it had happened before Independence, I'd feel differently about it, I suppose, but why defend something that doesn't belong to one?"

"Have you lived out here long?"

"Long? My dear girl, we're third generation out here. Our parents were born here and so were we. We'd never *live* anywhere else!"

Arab moved restively in her bed. "Then you don't want to go back to England with Sammy?"

Sandra shrugged. "I might. It depends what he offers me. I wouldn't mind going home for a bit. Lucien has a house somewhere in England. It's been in his family since Tudor times and he likes to spend some of his time there. This time, though, he seems to have got stuck out here for longer than usual. It's this boring book he's writing. He spends his life researching it and talks of nothing else! I shall be glad when he's finished it and is snapped up by some university or other for a spell of teaching."

Arab was interested despite herself. She had never thought of Lucien as a teacher. "What does he teach?" she asked.

Sandra giggled. "The poor dear is rather limited really. He was offered a chair in African Studies somewhere in America, but he'd only just finished setting up some school or other in London. Drives him mad when it's said that Africa has no history! But not every university seems to agree with him!"

"The African universities ought to!" Arab maintained, distressed by Sandra's patronising tone.

"They do! But I don't encourage him to talk in that direction. It's time he made some real money, and that's to be got in America. If you get the opportunity, dear, try putting that into his head, will you?"

"I wouldn't dream of it!" Arab retorted. "I know nothing about it, and nor do you! Beside, I don't think money matters much to Lucien!"

"Too, too ingenuous, aren't you?" Sandra answered. "Money matters to us all. It will matter to Lucien all right once he's married to me. I'm an expensive kind of person to have around!"

Depression descended on Arab like a black cloud. It was the malaria, she told herself, not believing a word of it. She knew what was the matter with her. She was jealous! Stupidly, humiliatingly jealous! Sandra was right about one thing, though, she *was* ingenuous—ingenuous enough to have believed that Lucien had been genuinely interested in her, when all the time he was planning to marry Sandra Dark. And much joy he would have of that! She couldn't believe that anyone as fine as Lucien would fall for the dross of Sandra Dark. But he must have done. Nobody, not even Sandra, talked about marriage to a man unless they had been given some reason to do so.

"How soon do you expect to be getting married?"

Sandra spent a long moment admiring her own ankles, wiggling her feet back and forth. "We'll wait for Ruth to come back," she said. She stood up unhurriedly, smoothing her skirt down over her hips. "I take it, then, that you have no objection to my taking over your job?"

Arab raised a feeble smile. "Take what you like?"

Sandra raised her eyebrows and then, as hastily, lowered them again, smoothing out her brow with her fingers. "Thanks, I will," she said. "But it's nice to know that I have your permission." She glanced casually at Arab's angry face. "It may not be tactful to tell you so, my dear, but you're not looking your best at the moment. I didn't like the way Lucien looked at you when you were all dressed up in that golden frock at the dance, but I don't think I have anything to worry about after all, do you?"

Arab bravely met the naked dislike in the other woman's eyes. "Not a thing!" she muttered. "But you already know that!"

"I just wanted to make quite, quite sure," Sandra purred. She went over to the door and opened it, a slight smile on her lips. "Oh, by the way, Lucien asked me to take your passport downstairs to him. Jill couldn't find it among your things at the hotel."

"It's in my handbag," Arab told her. "What does he want it for?"

"Don't ask me!" Sandra exclaimed. "You'll have to ask him—when you next see him. I hear you've forbidden him to come into your bedroom!"

Arab reached out for her handbag, found her passport and flipped it on to the end of the bed.

"I don't want to see *anyone*!" she said.

But Sandra only smiled all the more. "I'll tell him," she promised. "I won't forget!" She picked up the passport and went out the door, closing it behind her with a firm, decisive snap.

* * *

It was two days before Arab was allowed downstairs. Her ankle hampered all her movements, making her awkward and fractious and quite unlike her usual self. Lucien had offered to carry her down the stairs, but she had flatly refused his help, preferring to hang on to the banisters with grim determination, lowering herself slowly down, one step at a time.

"Where are you going to sit?" Hilary demanded, charging up and down the stairs beside her. "You can lean on me! I won't let you fall—I promise I won't!"

"Thank you," said Arab, sounding much more grateful than she felt. "I feel so weak at the knees!"

Lucien watched her as she transferred one hand from the banisters to Hilary's willing shoulder, pausing for an anxious moment while she regained her precarious balance.

"This is ridiculous!" he exclaimed. He pushed Hilary to one side and swept Arab up into his arms, striding down the stairs with a set look on his face. "Independence is all very well," he added grimly, "but you don't begin to know your own limitations, little one!"

Arab hugged herself closer to him, telling herself that if her breathing was peculiar, it had nothing to do with Lucien's proximity.

"Don't you dare drop me!" she cautioned him. "You told me that when you frightened me, I'd stay frightened, and I am! Mind my foot!"

"Be still!" he retorted. He smiled straight into her eyes. "And you're not frightened! Contrary to whatever that vivid imagination of yours tells you, I don't go round frightening young women, not even those I have designs on!"

"Hush," she said, blushing. "Sandra will hear you!"

"Let her hear! Let the whole world hear!" He put her down carefully, keeping an arm about her to help her into the sitting room. "Are you coming out into the garden to talk to me?" he suggested.

"No," she said. "*No!* I want to watch them working. I—I suppose they are here?"

"Yes, they're here." Lucien did not sound pleased and Arab's heart sank. She wished she could explain that she would prefer to be in the garden with him, but she didn't trust herself anywhere within his vicinity. She had only to look at him, to want to be in his arms and to feel his lips on hers. And he didn't mean it! He was going to marry Sandra and his kisses rightfully belonged to her!

"Has Sammy said anything about my going back to England?"

The sardonic look in his eyes unsettled her. "Not to me," he replied. "You'd better ask him about it."

"Yes, I will. Only—" she gnawed at her lower lip— "you have my passport. What did you want it for?"

He frowned and she wished she hadn't asked. "Oh yes," he said, "Sandra brought it down the other day. I'd forgotten all about it."

Then why had he asked for it? She gave him a puzzled look, but she said nothing more. Instead she began to hobble through the door, making her way out to the old ruined harem quarters, where the photography sessions were taking place. Hilary supported her with more energy than flair on one side and, on the other, she grasped at the wall, a chair, or whatever was going, grunting with the exertion.

Jill saw her the moment she turned the corner. "Arab!" she shrieked. "I didn't know you were coming downstairs today. My poor love, has it been very bad?"

"Well," Arab smiled, "it hasn't been good!"

Jill seized her arm and placed it about her neck, almost carrying her over to the nearest chair. "I suppose you're going to stay and watch for a while?"

Arab nodded. "How's it going?"

Jill screwed up her face warningly. "My lady has talent," she answered. "I'm not sure what she has talent for yet, but—oh, boy!"

Arab laughed, feeling suddenly very much better. "You don't like her!" she accused.

"Honey, do you?"

125

"Lucien does," Arab said before she could stop herself.

Jill whistled softly under her breath. "It's possible Sammy will take her back to England with him," she murmured. "He's busy making up his mind about her—"

"But surely he knows whether she can model or not by this time?"

"Model, she certainly can," Jill answered. "Even when I do manage to get between her and the lens, I'm definitely put in the shade! Sammy's interest is—less exclusive, shall we say?"

"Oh," said Arab, and then again, "*oh!*"

"*Exactly*, my pet. Give her her due, she never does or says a thing out of place, but she has poor Sammy running round in circles." Jill looked mournful. "I'm afraid she has cut you out there, honey. Do you think you can bear it?"

"Jill!" Arab reproved her. "As a matter of fact," she added, "I thought you liked her. I—I didn't know that Sammy hadn't wanted to bring me out here. Thank you for saying you would look after me. If I'd known—"

"You might have listened to Auntie, instead of thinking she was being stuffy."

Arab chuckled. "Stuffy isn't the first adjective that occurs to me when I think of you," she retorted. "Seriously though, it was nice of you, Jill."

Jill shrugged her shoulders. "Why not? I like you, honey." She glanced at her watch. "Good lord, is that the time? I must go and change. Keep laughing, sweetie, it suits you!"

Although Arab had Hilary to talk to at intervals during the morning, she was soon bored watching the others work. For a while she interested herself in seeing how Sandra worked. She was a great deal more professional than she had supposed. Arab thought sourly that there would be far fewer retakes than there would have been if she had been the model. Jill had been right, too, when she had said that Sandra hogged the camera. She was clever about it, but one ended up looking at her and not at Jill, or the clothes they were both supposed to be showing. Sammy was ecstatic when he saw the results. "Take a rest, girls. We'll have another go later," he croaked at them. Then he came over and sat beside Arab.

"I'm sorry, Sammy, to have let you down," Arab began to apologise.

"Don't, don't. Am I to be angry when you've done me such a good turn? This Sandra could be built up into something great! What d'you think of my taking her back to England? She's a bit old for a beginner."

"She has something—"

"Something better than youth! Duckie, that's exactly what I'm telling myself! You see it too?"

Arab thought of Lucien, stifling her conscience with difficulty. "She's very lovely," she said stiffly.

Sammy flung his fat arms about her and kissed her on the cheek. "I knew you'd see it my way! Well, well, back to work!"

Arab stared after him as he hurried away from her. This was a new Sammy, she thought, one she hadn't seen before. She felt oddly nostalgic for the old Sammy, the morose Sammy she had known for so long. It was something else that she couldn't like Sandra for; she had no right to use people for her own advantage, even when it was someone like Sammy, who had been using people himself and throwing them away when he had finished with them for longer than Arab had been alive.

She sighed, now thoroughly bored, and wondered what Lucien was doing. She was all the more surprised, therefore, to see him coming across the old, weed-covered bathing pool.

"Had enough?" he asked her abruptly.

She bit her lip and nodded. "It's dull having nothing to do," she explained. "I feel utterly useless!"

His dark eyes observed her quietly. "Hilary tells me you used to work in an office?"

She was startled. "I took up modelling to escape from it," she said dryly.

"But you do type?"

She nodded again. "Yes. I'm not bad at shorthand either."

"Good," said Lucien. "You can start work for me this afternoon. If you'll come now, I'll tell you what I want you to do."

Arab could only wonder at her own meekness. She lumbered eagerly to her feet, excitement and interest fountaining up within her, and when he held out his hand to her, she took it gladly, hobbling along beside him with a pleased smile on her face.

CHAPTER NINE

LUCIEN was a fierce taskmaster. Arab had never worked so long and so consistently at anything before. Every moment that she was not either eating or resting, she seemed to be pounding the typewriter, transcribing Lucien's illegible scrawl into a series of neatly typed scripts of articles, one or two chapters of the book he was writing, and page upon page of closely written notes on all aspects of East African history.

There was no time for her to fret, and she was too proud to ask Sammy if he had arranged anything about her flying home. The days came and went and she applied herself wholeheartedly to the work in hand. Then one day Jill came out into the garden, where Arab was working, and threw herself down on the coarse grass beside her.

"Only two more days—think of that, Arab! I can't wait to get back to England and home! How about you?"

Arab stopped typing. "Only two more days! Are you sure?" Her brow creased into a worried frown. "No one has said anything to me. I was waiting for Sammy to broach the subject—because of Sandra—"

"Darling, Sammy doesn't think of anything but Sandra!"

Arab sighed. "I suppose I shall have to ask him this evening," she said with such marked reluctance that Jill looked at her with concern.

"Worried about being left behind, love?"

"In a way," Arab admitted. "My parents will expect me back for my birthday anyway, and I can't stay here for ever, can I? Lucien has been more than kind, but I can't stay here when you've gone, and I can't afford to stay at the hotel. But I must say that I don't relish a nine-hour flight with my ankle still in plaster either."

"Doesn't look as though you have much choice," Jill said. "Sammy must have kept your reservation."

"I suppose so. I shall have to go anyway. My visitor's permit runs out then and one has to remember that this is a foreign country, though it doesn't feel like one."

"Not to you," Jill answered swiftly. "You speak for yourself!"

Arab laughed. "I am! I wouldn't dream of keeping you here another moment, unless your beloved husband were here beside you."

"That might make me see things differently," Jill agreed, somewhat smugly, "but I find it a bit too hot for everyday living. I shall be quite pleased to see a bit of English drizzle."

"And slushy snow?"

Jill nodded with decision. "And winter clothes, and eating hot, well-buttered crumpets in front of the fire!"

Arab stared dreamily at the notes she was typing. "You're welcome," she said.

Hilary was much more sanguine about Arab's prospects when she joined the other two in the garden. "I can't think why you have to worry about everything all the time! Lucien says that now he's found a willing slave to work for him, he's not going to relinquish you easily!"

Arab blushed scarlet. "I wish you wouldn't repeat what your uncle says all the time!" she protested.

Hilary looked at her with interest. "I think he's right," she announced. "He says that you're so much in love with Africa that you don't want to go home."

Would that it were only Africa she was in love with! Arab turned grimly back to the typewriter, determined not to think about Lucien for two minutes put together. Surely that wasn't taxing her powers too much? But it seemed it was. His writing was a blur before her eyes, and when she did manage to decipher something about the richness of the Swahili culture, it recalled his enthusiasm for the subject so vividly that she felt winded and unable to continue.

"What's that about?" Hilary demanded. "You're looking at it as though you can't understand a word of it!"

"Yes," Jill put in, "do you have to do that now? Surely Lucien wouldn't object if you took half an hour off to relax with us?"

"I want to get it finished," Arab answered, her chin set in a stubborn line that her friend recognised all too well.

"But what's it about?" Hilary repeated.

"It's about Swahili poetry," Arab told her. "Did you know they were composing fine lyric poems, called *mashairi*, in medieval times?"

Hilary giggled. "We don't learn any of them at school," she said.

Arab frowned at her levity. "You would if your uncle had his way! It seems they wrote epic poems as well, called *tendi*." She consulted Lucien's notes. "They're still writing them today. In the old days, though, they used a kind of corrupted Arabic script and a lot of Arabic idiom as well. Goodness, there were whole chronicles written about Mombasa and Pate! Did you know that when the archaeologists started to look at the ruined cities of the East African coast they thought they were looking at Arab or Persian towns, but now they aren't so sure? They form a distinct variant among medieval Islamic patterns. They now think it more likely that there was already a fine African culture that was slowly Islamised—in fact it's as much Negro as Islamic."

Jill sat up on one elbow. "And you find that interesting?"

Arab nodded apologetically. "I'm going to learn Swahili," she said. "I want to read all these poems for myself."

"Good idea!" a masculine voice congratulated her. She turned swiftly, jarring her ankle against the table.

It made her feel even more angry with Lucien than she was already. What right had he to come creeping up and overhearing their conversation? She hadn't wanted him to know that she planned to learn Swahili, for what chance would she ever have of coming back to Africa? She had thought it would be something she could do in England that would form a tenuous link between herself and her memories of him, because there was nothing else left to build on. He belonged to Sandra, and she—she would never belong to anyone, but would go lonely all her days.

Lucien came and stood very close beside her, peering over her shoulder at what she was typing.

"'*Madaka ya nyamba ya zisahani Sasa walaliye wana wa nyuni,*'" he quoted softly. It sounded like liquid magic on his tongue.

"What does it mean?" Arab asked him, despite her best intentions.

"It means, 'Where once the porcelain stood in the wall niches Now wild birds nestle their fledglings'."

"Oh," said Arab, "it could be Gedi, only there weren't any birds there, were there? Still, it could have been Gedi." She wanted it to be, urgently, though she didn't know why. "I'd like it to be Gedi," she ended uncertainly, feeling foolish.

"It was actually written about Pate," Lucien answered her. "But it could have been Gedi." He smiled intimately into her eyes. "Human birds get the nesting urge too," he reminded her. "Perhaps that's what Gedi means to you?"

Arab's breath caught in the back of her throat. "If I had," she said when she could, "it wouldn't be anything to do with you!"

"No?" he taunted her. "I long ago learned never to listen to what a woman *says*, my dear. It's her actions that count!"

"Lucien!" she exclaimed. "You're not very gallant, are you?"

"More so than you deserve! How dare you deny

your own instincts! Youth doesn't excuse everything, Arab."

Jill stirred uneasily. "I feel decidedly *de trop*," she murmured. "Hilary and I will go and get ready for lunch."

Arab was scarcely aware of their going. She sat miserably in front of the typewriter, wondering how Lucien could be so cruel. It wasn't she who was denying anything—it was him! He was the one who had this understanding with Sandra!

Lucien pushed a handkerchief into her unwilling hand. He looked harassed and as uncertain as she felt. "I suppose you're going to cry now!" he said in goaded tones. "You'd better be prepared."

"I'm *not* going to cry!"

Lucien sat on the edge of the table and looked down at her. He looked as stern and as unyielding as she had ever seen him.

"If you're not going to cry, suppose you tell me what went wrong," he suggested.

"*Nothing* went wrong! We—we both agreed that an—an affair was not what we wanted, and that there wasn't any chance of anything else. Well, I've had time to think, and I don't think I would enjoy having an affair with anyone anyway. I think I must be the all or nothing kind. So I'm quite happy to settle for nothing—"

"You look happy!" he commented.

"I am happy!" she declared furiously. "It would take more than one kiss from you to disturb me, let me tell you—"

"Then I'll kiss you again!" His arms went round her and his lips descended on hers. When he had finished, he gave her a mocking smile of triumph. "Are you still undisturbed?"

"I *hate you*!"

His hands fell to his sides. "There are times when I do a pretty good job of hating myself," he admitted. "I'm sorry, Arab."

"It doesn't matter," she said dully.

"I think it does. I'm beginning to think an affair wouldn't suit me either. Will you stay here a week or two longer, Arab, and finish typing up my notes for me?"

She shook her head. "The others are going back to England—there's my birthday, you see. My parents expect me to share it with them. They—they've made plans for what we're going to do. I can't disappoint them now."

Lucien stared at her for a long moment. "Sammy is taking Sandra to England with him. That's what I wanted your passport for, to get your visitor's permit extended. You won't be able to fly back with the others, Arab."

"But I have to! I can't stay here!"

"Can't you, little one?"

"I've told you! I won't stay in your house without another woman being here. I'm—I'm sorry, Lucien." Another thought struck her. "Sammy can't leave me stranded here, can he?"

"Not if he wants to stay alive!" Lucien assured her with a hint of a smile. "But I hope you'll stay, all the same. When you're twenty-one I'll feel better about forcing a decision on you that you seem far too young to make at the moment!"

Arab clenched her fists. "I shan't change my mind!"

"Circumstances change—"

"But people's feelings don't!" she exclaimed sharply.

He smiled at her, his eyes suddenly warm and amused. "Is that a promise?" he asked her.

She tried to stop the blush that crept up her cheeks. "Don't you think you ought to ask someone else that?" she countered with dignity.

He put a hand on the nape of her neck so that she couldn't escape his searching glance. "Whom would you suggest I ask?"

"S—Sandra," she stammered.

His grasp tightened on her neck. "Sandra has nothing to do with you," he ripped into her. "Or do you resent her success with Sammy Silk?"

"Oh, but," Arab said before she had thought, "that doesn't mean a thing! She only wants to make sure of a job with Sammy. She's waiting—" She broke off, appalled at how easily she might have broken the other girl's confidence. "I mean—"

"Yes?"

"I mean she's in love with someone else," Arab ended dismally.

His hand fell away from her. "Oh, Arab, spare me that! Is it likely that Sandra would confide in someone like you? She's practically old enough to be your mother! Nor does she have much time for anyone as ingenuous as you are, as you've heard her say yourself. No, my dear, you may be too young to be sure of your own emotions, but don't try to shift the responsibility on to anyone else. You have exactly one week, my love, to sort yourself out, and not a moment longer!"

Arab gritted her teeth together. "I shall be back in England then," she muttered with a toss of her head.

"Perhaps."

"I told you! I'm going to celebrate my birthday with my parents and—and that's in a week's time. So you see—"

"One week!" he repeated.

He strode off into the house as though he couldn't stand her company an instant longer. Arab sat on in the garden for a long time, exhausted by the interview with Lucien and, damn it all, she believed she was going to cry after all! She found she was still holding his handkerchief and, holding it close against her cheek, the tears brimmed over and ran unchecked down her face. *He knew*, she thought, he knew he had only to touch her and she was helpless against him. He probably thought she would share him with Sandra, and would still think that Sandra was none of her business. He had lived too long in a Moslem environment to see anything wrong with that! But how dared he blame it on her? No, she decided wearily, the sooner she went back to England the better. In England, her parents would make a fuss of her and she would forget all about him. She sniffed pathetically and dabbed at her face with his handkerchief. Sandra was welcome to him! They were very well matched. They were both adult and sophisticated and would doubtless understand if they each had less than an exclusive interest in the other! Whereas she was young and foolish and wanted nothing else than the whole of Lucien's love. And a lot of chance she had of that, with only her *gamin*, ragamuffin ways and charm to help her. She might as well make up her mind to that, no matter how much it hurt.

If she was still red-eyed and a little tearful at lunch-time, everyone was far too tactful to remark on it. Only Hilary asked her if her ankle was hurting her and, when she admitted that it was, began to tell her uncle that Arab had had enough of sitting round the house. "You ought to take her to see the Giriama dancers," she said, looking quaintly up at him. "Typing all your stuff doesn't take her mind off the pain!"

Lucien shot a glance across the table at Arab.

"Perhaps it isn't only her ankle that's hurting," he said.

But Hilary only laughed at this suggestion. "Her head has stopped aching," she told him with an authoritative air. "One's head only aches when one actually has malaria, but Arab hasn't got it now, and I see that she takes her paludrin every day, so she probably won't get it again."

Lucien raised his eyebrows. "All right," he agreed. "I'll make arrangements to go and see the dancing."

Arab lay on the sofa, striving not to think about the pain in her ankle. It was the hottest part of the afternoon, when the very air itself seemed to be catching its breath before the cooler time of the evening. What, she wondered, was she going to say to Sammy? The same question had been turned over and over in her mind ever since lunch, and she couldn't put it off for very much longer because Sammy would soon call it a day. They had finished the whole assignment a day early and the next day had been declared a celebratory holiday. If she didn't see him this evening, she might not see him at all.

There was a strange noise in the hall and Arab turned her head, trying to make up her mind whether she ought to go and investigate it. It was such an effort moving anywhere with this lump of plaster on the end of her leg! The door into the sitting room opened slowly and a totally strange woman stuck her head into the room.

"Hullo," said Arab.

The woman jumped, then smiled, coming right over to the sofa and looking down at Arab with amused, familiar eyes. She was really very like Lucien.

"You must be Arab," she said in a delightful, contralto voice. "The one who didn't know enough—"

"To take off her shoes!" Arab finished for her.

The stranger laughed. "Hilary was quite right—you're nice! But, forgive me, has Lucien been beating you up? You look a little the worse for wear!"

"I broke my ankle," Arab explained.

The amused eyes twinkled at her. "I thought Lucien had been less resourceful than usual for a moment, and that was the only way he could get you to stay!"

Arab veiled her eyes behind her long eyelashes. "I don't know that he wants me to stay," she said.

The eyes lost none of their amusement. "My dear, I'm sorry. I didn't mean to pry into what is, after all, your own business. I should have introduced myself, instead of embarrassing you, but then the Manners never did think before they spoke! I'm Ruth Dark."

"Does Hilary know you're here?"

"No, not yet. You're the only person I've seen. I received this odd letter from Lucien." Ruth Dark hesitated almost imperceptibly. "Do you know my sister-in-law?"

Arab nodded, saying nothing, in case it all came flooding out, even the details of how Lucien affected her and how he only had to appear for her to feel weak at the knees and short of breath, and a lot of other unpleasant things besides!

"She's an unhappy sort of person," Ruth continued. "What is all this about her taking your job? Did you agree, or were you pushed into it?"

"I agreed," Arab said. "Sort of. I didn't have much option really. I could hardly model the clothes myself with a broken ankle and washed-out with malaria." She broke off, aware of an underlying bitterness in her words. "This was the big opportunity of my career, and I should have minded very much, but I didn't. I thought I was heading straight for the top! But I don't think I'm a very ambitious person after all."

Ruth sat down on the leather chair opposite the sofa, crossing her legs in front of her with an easy elegance that Arab wished Sandra could have witnessed. If Sandra's legs were admirable, they were quite put in the shade by those of Lucien's sister.

"Ambition is a funny thing," she remarked. "I never wanted to do anything much when my husband was alive. It was only after he died that I found I had this driving urge to achieve something—and not just anything! It had to be something as worthwhile as what Lucien was doing. Does that seem ridiculous to you?"

"Oh no!" Arab exclaimed.

Ruth smiled. "A lot of people do. Most think I ought to devote myself to Hilary and not gad about the countryside. Lucien encouraged me to do my thing though right from the start. Without him, I never could have done it!"

Arab's eyes became soft and dreamy. "I've been typing his notes for him," she said.

A chuckle was her only answer from Ruth and she became guiltily aware that she had sounded exactly like a stage-struck teenager. She tried to regain more solid ground by rushing into an explanation as to how she had been a shorthand-typist before she had been a model.

"Whatever made you admit such a thing?" Ruth demanded. "My dear girl, Lucien will *never* let you go! Nor will I, come to that! I don't suppose you're interested in anthropology? I have a mountain of notes that all need putting in order. Enough to keep you here for weeks!"

"But I don't want to stay here for weeks!" Arab wailed

There was another telling chuckle from Ruth. "Of course you don't," she said comfortably. "I expect you're longing to get home. By the way," she added, "what are all those people doing in the garden? Sandra looks very much at home in their midst."

Arab made a face, an expression she had caught from Hilary. Ruth recognised it immediately and burst into laughter. "She has made a hit with you!" she drawled. She swivelled round in her chair, leaning forward to see better out of the window. "I hope my daughter hasn't been sharing her prejudices with you. My word, poor Sandra!"

"She looks as though she's doing all right to me!" Arab said grimly.

"Perhaps." Ruth blinked at the picture of her sister-in-law drawing Sammy Silk's arm through hers. Sammy was scowling and Sandra pathetically eager to please him. "Poor Sandra!" Ruth said again.

"Oh, but," Arab began, "she hasn't any long-term plans in the rag trade. She—she's coming back. She wants to look at Lucien's house in England."

Ruth's eyes widened. "*Lucien's* house? That's rubbish, my dear. Our parents live in the only house the Manners have in England, and they and Sandra are like chalk and cheese! I doubt very much if she'll even visit them!"

"But she said—" Arab sounded flustered and a bit hurt. "I suppose she was trying to be kind—"

Ruth flashed her a quick look. "Sandra has never bothered to be kind. It would never occur to her. But I must say, this fellow doesn't look very kind either. I hope Sandra doesn't get hurt!"

"Sammy wouldn't hurt a fly!"

"You may be right." Ruth turned her back on the garden. "It looks to me as though Sandra may have to pay dearly for taking your job. Is this Sammy married?"

Arab shook her head. "He's a widower. Jill is the only married person in the outfit. She's been staying here with me ever since I broke my ankle," she said hastily. "I'd have gone back to the hotel otherwise."

The twinkle came back into Ruth's eyes. "Can you stagger out into the garden?" she asked. "I think I'd like to meet your friends. Hilary's letters didn't say much about them."

"They wouldn't!" Arab retorted. "Every paragraph would begin with 'Lucien says—', just like her conversation!"

"You couldn't be more wrong," Ruth defended her daughter. "Every other paragraph began with 'Arab says'! So there!"

Arab blushed scarlet, wondering what she could have said that would have been interesting to Hilary. "I hope I haven't been misquoted," she said in a stifled voice.

"Oh, I shouldn't think so," Ruth teased her. "Hilary is almost always accurate, especially when she likes the people concerned. I think she's quite astute for her age."

Arab wished she knew what Hilary had said about her, but as she couldn't very well ask, she struggled on to her feet and began to propel herself across the room towards the french windows. Sammy had shaken off Sandra and was standing a little apart from the others, staring gloomily at a hibiscus flower. Arab, who had never looked at him in any other light other than as an employer, thought suddenly that despite his weight and build there was a romantic air about him. He had a dissipated, Byronic look that might appeal to Sandra. Was that what Ruth had seen? Arab felt a stirring of interest, but her spirits refused to respond. It was too good to be true! Sandra would work on Sammy for her own ends, but she would be back to reclaim Lucien as soon as she was ready, and there was nothing that Arab could do about it.

"I thought you'd be rejoicing, Sammy," she said to his back. "I want you to meet Lucien's sister."

He turned, frowning. "Oh yes?" He dismissed Ruth with a scowl. "I have to talk to you, Arab. We're flying to Nairobi tomorrow evening, ready to fly home the day after." His frown became directly addressed to her. "You're not coming with us. I'm taking Sandra instead."

"But you can't!"

His mouth turned down at the corners. "You must have seen it coming!" he said angrily. "Sandra is of more use to me than you are in your present state. Besides, you've got yourself a comfy job for the moment. Why not settle for that?"

"Because I came out here with you and I mean to go home with you!"

"You can follow, when you're feeling better. It isn't the end of the world, duckie. Am I an ogre now, for you to be looking at me like that?"

Arab winced. "You don't understand! I *can't* stay here!"

"You'll have to! There isn't another seat on the plane. This is the tourist season and all the planes are full—"

"Why can't Sandra wait for a seat?" Arab pleaded.

"Because I want to work with her as soon as we get back to England," Sammy declared brutally. "Heaven knows when you'll be working again! You look wretched after that bout of malaria and you're so thin, your bones are showing. I'm doing you a favour, love. This work was never really in your line anyway."

Arab threw all caution to the winds, her temper rising. "I suppose I can thank Sandra for that last judgement too?" she suggested.

Sammy glared at her. "She noticed you were looking poorly. Surely you don't resent that? What's the matter with you? Always you've shown far too little temperament and now, when we can do without it, you look mad enough to be a full-blown star!"

"I *won't* be left behind!"

Sammy shrugged his shoulders. "If you can find yourself a seat, come by all means!"

Arab went very white. She limped away from him as fast as she could, blindly looking about her for some kind of refuge from his cruelty. How could she stay? It had not been fair to Lucien in the first place, when he had taken her in because she was ill, but to do this to him was too much. It put them both in a false position. And what on earth were her parents going to say?

Jill watched her move away by herself, feeling bitter that Sammy should have found it necessary to hurt anyone so vulnerable. She thought she had a very good idea of how Arab was feeling, but at least she would be safe with Lucien Manners. He wasn't the kind of man to take advantage of someone as innocent, so downright *young* as Arab! She sighed and went over to her.

"He told you at last, honey?"

Arab nodded. "I know it's his fault, but somehow I can't help blaming Sandra even more. She'd better not come anywhere near me this evening—I could tear her limb from limb!"

Jill suppressed a smile. "You look fierce enough to do it, but I fancy that she can run faster than you can at the moment!"

"Just as well!" Arab grunted.

"Yes, that's all very well, but weren't your parents going to meet you, hon? Why don't you write them a nice long letter and I'll give it to them the moment we arrive. They'll be worried about you and it will ease their mind if I can tell them you are all right."

"I'm not all right."

"Of course you are, love. I've just been talking to Hilary's mum. Now, she's a darling—quite unlike that sister-in-law of hers! She's agreed to take over where I leave off as far as you're concerned, so I'll be able to tell your parents that at least."

"Oh no!" said Arab.

"What's the matter? Don't you like her?"

Arab nodded helplessly. "Of course I do! But I wish you could get it out of your head that I need a permanent bodyguard. I shall be *twenty-one* in one week's time!"

But Jill refused to take any such protest seriously. "More a nurse than a bodyguard!" she smiled. "You keep a tight hold of nurse, my pet, or you will be finding something worse!"

"It couldn't be worse! What will Lucien think? How can Sammy do this to me?" Arab's voice rose in a crescendo of humiliation. "I don't even know how long I have to foist myself on him!"

Jill looked smug. "But that's what I'm trying to tell you, if you'd only listen, instead of feeling sorry for yourself. You're staying here from now on as Mrs. Dark's guest. It has nothing to do with Lucien. And that, my hot-headed friend, was *her* idea, so don't go blaming me for it!"

"Really?" Arab's relief knew no bounds. She saw Ruth Dark standing by herself on the other side of the lawn and, grasping Jill by the hand, she began the painful journey across the grass to her side.

"You manage that ankle of yours pretty well!" Ruth congratulated her.

Arab took a deep breath. "I'm sorry," she burst out. "Sammy shouldn't have done it! I'll go on the first available plane, I promise you!"

Ruth put her hands on her shoulders and kissed her on the cheek. "I'll love having you! And unless my dear sister-in-law has changed a lot, I daresay this was all her idea and that poor Sammy is merely being played along. The joke is that Sammy looks quite like a shark and big game fishing is outside Sandra's usual league." She tried to look penitent and failed. "I'm not usually catty," she added. "It's one of the less delightful side-effects of being anywhere near Sandra, I'm afraid!"

"And you don't mind?" Arab insisted, still white with misery.

Ruth's eyes twinkled mercilessly. "It's one of the reasons I came flying home," she assured her. "Hilary wrote that Lucien had said—"

It was Jill who groaned. "Oh no! Mrs. Dark, I'm devoted to your daughter, but her hero-worship for your brother is very hard to bear!"

"That's nothing," said Ruth. She grinned, looking very like Lucien indeed. "You haven't heard *me* quoting my brother yet! I hero-worship him too! And I have strong hopes of another convert!" She chuckled. "*Hilary* says—" she began.

CHAPTER TEN

ARAB hadn't seen Hilary all day. All afternoon she had been hoping that the child would come and find her, because she wanted her to go with her to Malindi's minute airport to see the others off on the first leg of their journey to England. She had decided that she had to go, although she could easily have missed seeing either Sammy or Sandra ever again. But Jill had wanted her to be there to wave her goodbye, and Arab hadn't had the heart to refuse.

Ruth had proved to be an easy hostess. She had kept Arab entranced with her stories of her doings in Ethiopia. At breakfast, she had told them all about a young girl who had walked a hundred miles to obtain a love potion to give to her ancient husband.

"That's nothing!" Hilary had said with contempt. "There's a man who lives near here who has eighty wives. He's a witch-doctor!"

Her mother had laughed. "He sounds a successful one!" she had agreed.

Even Lucien had listened closely to his niece's romancing about this man. "Where did you hear about him?" he had asked her.

Hilary had grinned. "They were talking about him in the African market," she had said. "They have a very good line in gossip down there."

It was shortly after breakfast that Hilary had disappeared. Ruth and Lucien had gone out for the day with friends.

"Take a taxi to the airport," Lucien had bidden Arab. "We'll pick you up there and bring you home."

"You don't have to go if you don't want to," she had murmured, anxious not to be a nuisance.

"Ruth wishes to go," he had answered. "I think she has something to say to Sandra."

Arab had frozen. "All right," she had said, "I'll see you there. I'll go in the same taxi as Jill."

"I thought you might," he had drawled.

The house had been very quiet after they had gone. Arab had spent the morning working. Lucien had left her a whole lot of notes on the ancient trading of the Indian Ocean, long before the European had made his mark on that area. It was a fascinating saga of brave men, ships, gold, silver and ivory. East African metals were superior to those of India and the best swords were those which were fashioned from them. Later, when the Europeans had taken over most of the trade, they became convinced that their civilisation had always been superior to those of the Indian Ocean. The many surviving monuments in India had been an uncomfortable reminder that this was not so, but along the East Coast of Africa the cities had fallen into ruin and had been swallowed up by the surrounding vegetation. European superiority had reigned supreme.

But even this story, with the side issue of the slave trade coming and going to reveal the darker side of ancient trading, failed to enthral Arab as it usually did. The house was too silent.

She had her solitary lunch to the accompaniment of the wireless. She tried asking the African servant where Hilary was, but he didn't understand her question. By the time she had finished her meal she was really worried. She told herself that Hilary would be out somewhere with Ayah, but she couldn't rid herself of the feeling that something was wrong.

With some difficulty she crossed the garden, her book in her hand, intending to find a shady place in the ruined harem which she hoped would be cooler than inside the house. It took her a long time to hobble over the rough ground and once she nearly fell. She recovered herself, ruefully staring down at the plaster on her foot, when a lazy call from under a nearby mango tree made her look up. She was astonished to see Ayah reclining on the ground, smiling broadly at her.

"Ayah!" she exclaimed. "Where's Hilary?"

Ayah yawned sleepily. "Memsahib Kjana has her mother to see to her today," she answered somewhat huffily.

"But Memsahib Dark has gone out with the Bwana!"

Ayah's eyes grew round with panic. "You sure of that? You sure?"

Arab nodded. "I haven't seen Hilary since breakfast," she said. "There was no sign of her when the others left."

"But where she gone? She very naughty girl to go without telling Ayah. I have something to say to that girl when she get back!"

"Yes, but where could she have gone?"

Ayah shook her head, her eyes now starting out of her head. "She a bad girl! Never say to Ayah where she go! She take a bus somewhere! She get Ayah into bad trouble!"

Arab sighed. She remembered how she had first come across Hilary at Mambrui. The child had been playing truant on that occasion. No doubt there had been many other occasions! But surely, now her mother was home, there was no need for Hilary to go off by herself in search of adventure.

"We'll have to find her!" she said aloud to Ayah.

"I don't know where she gone!"

"I don't know either," Arab said patiently. "Let's try and think where she might have gone."

"I not know!"

Arab sat down heavily on a piece of broken wall. "If I could only drive!" she wished uselessly. "I feel so helpless!"

"She come back," Ayah muttered. She settled herself more comfortably against the trunk of the mango tree and closed her eyes.

"*No!* It won't do. We can't leave an eleven-year-old running around on her own! Anything might happen to her!" A pang of anxiety made her recoil from her plastered foot and she stood up with sudden decision. "I shall find someone who can drive!" she declared. "I'll telephone to the hotel."

This was easier said than done, but eventually Jill came to the phone.

"I'm packing, love. What is it?"

"Hilary has disappeared!"

"How long?"

Arab sighed with relief. It was something just to share her anxiety with another person and Jill could be relied upon to understand without asking a whole lot of useless questions.

"It's awful!" she said. "She might have gone anywhere! And I can't go and look for her with my foot. Jill, you couldn't drive me, could you?"

There was a brief silence at the other end. "I would, honey, but you know I can't drive!"

"Oh, Jill! You *must* be able to!"

"No, truly, I never have driven anything, not even a bicycle! You'll have to get someone else, pet. Wouldn't Sandra—" Her voice trailed off as though even she could see that Sandra was unlikely to spend the day looking for her truant niece. "I'll ask the French boys!" she suggested with a flash of inspiration. "Will you hold on?"

"Yes," said Arab.

There followed an endless wait. Arab pulled a chair over to the telephone, almost tripping herself up as she did so. She sat down, with her leg stuck out in front of her, and wondered that she had managed to get the plaster so dirty in such a short time.

"Are you there, *ma belle*?"

"Jacques! Oh, Jacques! I thought you might have gone back to work—"

"Not yet, *ma mie*. Your friend Jill said you wished to speak to me. Have you changed your mind, Bella?"

"Changed my mind?" Arab repeated. "Oh, that!" She was immediately embarrassed. "Well, no, I'm afraid not. I'm beginning to think that stardust isn't much in my line. But, Jacques—?"

"Yes, I am still listening," he assured her.

"Hilary has disappeared. Are you doing anything?"

"But of course I am doing something. When your friend came to find me I was teaching the most beautiful woman in the whole of East Africa to swim in the pool here. My true love has rejected me, but I am not one to mope alone with my broken heart! Did you think I would?"

"Idiot!" Arab said with real affection. "Seriously though, will you drive me if I go and look for her?"

He hesitated. "Where will you go?"

"To Mambrui," she said. "She might go there. There's a bus she could have taken that goes from the harbour."

"*D'accord,*" he agreed immediately. "Do I come and pick you up? I and Jean-Pierre have hired a Mini-Moke between the two of us. If he is not using it just now, I shall be with you in about ten minutes."

Arab clutched the telephone to her ear. "Thank you," she whispered.

"It is nothing. I am glad that you ask me to do this for you." She could hear that he was smiling. "I could wish that it was something more valorous, you know, something to make you lose your heart to me. But I am the realist, you understand, and your heart, it no longer belongs to you! *Calme-toi, petite!* We shall find her very soon. You will see!"

"I hope so," Arab sighed.

She went out into the drive to wait for him, forgetting her original intention of changing first so that she would be ready to go straight to the airport the instant Hilary was found. She was wearing her old, frayed jeans again, because she could get them easily over the plaster cast on her foot. At the moment she was so hot that they stuck to her flesh. If only Lucien were here, she thought, he would know where to find Hilary! She longed for him to appear, to sweep her along in his train as he took charge with all his usual confidence. But of course he did nothing of the kind. The trees rustled over her head, but otherwise there was no sound to be heard anywhere.

Jacques came storming up the drive, drawing up right beside her. He grinned at her, raising his eyebrows at her jeans.

"Can you get in by yourself?" he asked her.

Arab made a half-hearted attempt to do so, wishing she had remembered to change while she had waited for him. "I don't think I can," she said.

He jumped out of the Moke and lifted her bodily into the passenger seat, arranging the foot on a cushion on the running board that went all round the cockpit of the car.

"The roads are murder," he warned her. "Shall I go and look for the child by myself?"

"No, I must go!" she insisted. "Jacques, you don't think anything bad could have happened to her?"

"To Hilary? Never!"

"I wish I could be so sure!" she muttered. "I'm really worried! She hasn't been seen by anyone since breakfast time. She *is* only eleven years old!"

"Is there no one else to worry about her?" Jacques asked in matter-of-fact tones. "What about the uncle?"

"Lucien is out. So is Hilary's mother. We all thought she had gone somewhere with her *ayah*."

"I see." He shrugged. "Very well. Mambrui, here we come!"

The road, as he had said, was much rougher than she had remembered it. It was one thing to drive along such a road oneself, it was another to be driven. However careful Jacques was, her ankle came in for some rough treatment and, by the time they had crossed the bridge and had started along the worst part of the road to Mambrui, her foot ached abominably.

Mambrui was practically deserted. A few women sat in the doorways of the houses, but there was no one that Arab felt she could ask if they had seen Hilary. Then, just when she had begun to despair, she saw the old man who had taken such exception to her entering the tomb of their holy man in her shoes. Her first instinct was to hope that he hadn't seen her, but then she knew that she would have to ask him, for he at least had seen Hilary before. He even spoke a few words of English, though he had been reluctant to use it. She signalled to Jacques to stop the Mini-Moke and, immediately, half a dozen small boys swarmed round them, hoping to collect a few coppers from the strangers. Arab chose one who looked lively and intelligent and asked him to go over to the old man and tell him that she wished to speak to him.

The old man shook his head, refusing to so much as lift his head. His prayer beads rattled through his fingers in time to the nasal chant of the names of Allah that the old man kept up without pausing. Arab beckoned to the boy to come back to her and spent some time explaining what had happened before and why the old man disliked her.

"Tell him that I am sorry—that I didn't know," she said to the boy. "I was very sorry to offend him—and see, I have been punished for it, because now I have broken my ankle, as he can see for himself!"

The boy went back to the old man, repeating all she had said in Swahili with a great deal of laughter. Finally, the old man wheezed out a laugh too and stood up, wincing at the pain in his bones as he moved slowly over to the Mini-Moke. He put out a bony hand and poked the plaster on Arab's foot, cackling with glee at her explanation of her accident.

"I have not seen the Memsahib Kjana," he said finally in English. "I know the child. She is fond of stories and I have told her many in the past." He lifted his head and his eyes met Arab's briefly. "I will ask at the mosque," he said.

Jacques was frankly impatient as they watched the old man creep away down the narrow street, feeling the rough sides of the houses as he went to keep his balance.

"That's the last we've seen of him!" he grunted. "Shall I go after him?"

But Arab shook her head. "He will come back. It was courteous of him to come over. Last time I was here, I did a dreadful thing—"

Jacques grinned at her. "I heard," he murmured. "How were you to know?"

"Lucien said I should have found out about local customs before flinging myself into breaching them," Arab said ruefully.

"*Lucien said*! I see Hilary is not the only one to quote the great man!"

Arab blushed at his teasing. "He was right, though," she observed, forgetting how cross she had been when he had said it to her.

"Did you tell him so?" Jacques asked, a wicked glint in his eyes.

"No," Arab admitted. "He's quite conceited enough!"

The Frenchman chuckled. "There is hope for you yet, Bella, if you can still see that!"

Arab lifted her chin. "I don't know what you mean!" she declared.

Happily she was rescued from his giving her any explanation by the old man coming back towards them, still chanting as the beads slipped through his fingers.

"She has been seen," he panted, as he came up to them. "She is not here, but it is thought that she has gone to the Swahili village on the other side of Malindi. It was said in the market place that she has gone to see the witch-doctor—"

"*Alone*?"

The old man's eyes, blue with blindness, stared dully into hers. "The Kjana is alone. She speaks with the witch-doctor about her friend."

Arab gasped, blushing fiercely. "About me?"

The old man patted her plaster cast, neighing with silent laughter, and then tottered off down the street, collapsing into the nearest doorway. His grizzled hair had been cut so short that his black scalp gleamed in the sunlight, damp from the effort he had made. Arab wondered how old he was. She thought he must be a great age and she was glad that they were no longer enemies.

"Do you know this village?" she asked Jacques.

He gave her an odd look. "Do you intend to go there?" he countered. "It sounds to me as though Hilary knows what she's doing. She won't come to any harm!"

Arab looked stubborn. "She might!" She threaded her fingers together nervously. "I'd never forgive myself if anything happened to her!"

Jacques shook his head at her. "She's not your responsibility, Bella!"

"I think she is!"

He shrugged his shoulders with a Gallic gesture. "My dear, have you thought what you are doing? You are too beautiful to give up your work, did you know that? As a model, you have prestige, and dresses like the one you wore to the dance—" He broke off, annoyed to see that she was laughing at him. "Well? What is so funny?"

"You are!" she giggled. "You don't know anything about being a model!"

"It brought you out here—to me!"

"Not to you!" Arab frowned. "And this was the best thing that's happened to me. Mostly, it's nothing but changing clothes, rushing round in taxis in a constant fever in case one is late for an appointment, and talking clothes, clothes, *clothes*, until you wish they'd never been invented! If it isn't clothes, it's dieting, because most of us have to worry about our figures all the time too. At the end of a day, I could often scream with boredom!"

"I don't believe you! Why did you become a model if this is true?"

Arab grinned. "Because being a shorthand-typist was worse, or so I thought. Recently, since coming out here, I've begun to wonder if I'm really cut out for the independent, liberated life, but there isn't much choice in the end, is there?"

Jacques looked serious. "*Chérie*, let's leave Hilary to her own devices! Come with me, and I shall persuade you that you will find happiness with me. I earn very good money, I assure you! There would be no need for you to work any more. All you would have to be is my golden goddess, and I should adore you, no?"

Arab wriggled uncomfortably. "But I'm not a golden goddess," she objected.

"Today, you are my Cinderella, full of family worries that are nothing to do with you! But we wave a wand, and you are dressed for the Ball. I have seen you when you are beautiful! You must not forget that!"

"That's not the real me," she said. She was irresistibly reminded of the time when Lucien had kissed her in the House of the Scissors. He had said it was her ridiculous jeans that had first made him want to kiss her. He hadn't required the glamour of a golden dress! Tears started into her eyes. If only it were he and not Jacques who was beside her now!

"It's real enough for me!"

"Please don't!" Arab said abruptly.

"But, Bella, it is silly for you to cry for the moon when the stars are all yours for the taking!"

"I don't happen to want any stars!"

"Did you dislike my kisses so much?"

Arab nodded, chewing at her lower lip. "I'm sorry, Jacques."

He spread his hands out before him. "I am a very stubborn man," he warned her. "You will grow to like my kisses."

"No, I won't. Please, Jacques, don't go on about it! You don't know me at all, and I don't think you would like me very much if you did. I'm just ordinary me and I don't want to be anybody else." She shifted her foot with immense care. "Certainly not Madame Jacques Bouyer!" she added.

"How about Mrs. Lucien Manners?" he drawled.

Arab winced. "Lucien isn't looking for a wife," she answered. "And I don't think I should be very happy with anything else." She laughed shortly. "I shall get over it—I hope!"

Arab shook her head. "I'm sorry," she said again. "But not with me?"

She was dismayed to see the tightness about Jacques' mouth and she wished that she hadn't had to refuse him. Jill had said he was looking for a flirtation, but he had wanted a wife after all. What a pity she couldn't feel the same way about him! How simple everything would be, if she could only have fallen in love with Jacques Bouyer! She waited for him to start the engine, but he sat in the driving seat with his hands on the wheel, making no effort to move. After a while Arab became restive. She tried a light laugh that didn't quite come off. "Hadn't we better be going?" she said.

Jacques gave her an angry look. "I wouldn't have come if it was only a chauffeur you were wanting!" he said sourly. "If you want me to drive you around, you'll have to pay me for it."

"Pay you?" Arab exclaimed. "What on earth are you talking about?"

"You know very well, *ma mie*. Shall we say a kiss a mile? Or I shall leave you here to get home by yourself!"

Arab controlled her temper with difficulty. "Don't be ridiculous! I have to be at the airport at five!"

"You should have thought of that before!" Jacques mocked her with a cruel twist to his mouth.

Arab took a deep breath. "All right," she said. "A kiss a mile it is. Now let's get going. I'm worried about Hilary and I want to get to her as quickly as possible!"

She noted the surprised look on Jacques' face, followed by a quick gleam of triumph. "I had not expected you to be so—amenable," he murmured. "Perhaps I need not have offered you marriage after all?"

Arab only grunted. She was busy thinking about how she was going to get out of paying him. It should be easy enough, she decided. She would put him off until they arrived at the airport and then there would be too many people around for it to matter!

"Please, let's go!"

Reluctantly, Jacques turned the ignition key and backed the Mini-Moke towards the sea, roaring the engine as he changed gear and sped through the narrow streets, scattering people and animals in all directions with a lack of concern for others that jarred harshly on Arab's nerves.

By the time they arrived at the Swahili village, Arab could only think of one thing: the gnawing pain in her ankle that was growing steadily by the minute. Jacques parked the Mini-Moke in the shade of a tree and she sat there, without moving, for a long moment, hoping that the pain was going to subside. It soon became obvious that it was there to stay. The sweat formed in drops on her face and her clothes felt tight and damp.

"Will you help me out, please," she asked Jacques.

He lifted her out of her seat and set her down on her feet. "I think I'll take the first instalment of my payment now," he began.

Arab pulled herself away from him. "I'm too hot and sticky!" She looked about her. "Have you ever been here before?"

"What for?" Jacques countered cautiously.

Arab glanced at him sharply. She knew quite certainly that he had been to the village before and that he didn't want to tell her about it. Oh well, she thought, it was none of her business what he did! But it gave her an uncomfortable feeling that she didn't know Jacques as well as she thought she had. She turned away from him, idly watching a bevy of small children who had gathered about the car.

"Tour, *memsahib*? Tour of village? I best guide!"

Arab's eyes met those of a small boy and she pointed to him. "*Jambo*," she said to him, pleased with her one word of Swahili.

"*Jambo, memsahib*. You want to see the village?"

Arab nodded. "I'm looking for a girl who might have come here today. Have you seen her?"

The boy's head fell forward and he shuffled his feet in the dust, pretending not to have understood her. Arab sighed. There was nothing for it, she thought, but to make the tour of the village and hope to see Hilary on the way.

"She's eleven years old," she said slowly and clearly, in case the boy hadn't understood her. "She has yellow hair," she added.

The boy looked up, his eyes wide. "Tour, *memsahib*?"

Arab looked over her shoulder at Jacques. He had got back into the Mini-Moke and had pulled out a paperback which he was studying with interest. Arab felt quite exasperated. It would have been easy enough for him to have made the tour of the village, whereas she wasn't sure that she would be able to walk that far.

"Are you coming?" she asked Jacques.

"No," he replied.

Her guide was surprisingly helpful. He told her to stand still where she was and, in a few seconds he was back with a stout walking stick in his hand. With the help of the stick and the boy's shoulder, Arab found she could swing along fairly well. She might even have enjoyed it had it not been for the nagging ache in her foot which obstinately refused to go away.

Everybody in the village was friendly. There was the sound of laughter echoing round the trees and there were no suspicious eyes watching everything she did such as she had noticed at Mambrui. Her guide showed her the cashew trees, where small boys hurried to pick the nuts and toast them over mangrove charcoal, urging her to try them. He pointed out the cups at the top of the palm trees to catch the palm juice that is the basis of the *tembo* drink that they all drank with relish whenever they could.

"Have you a witch-doctor here?" Arab asked her guide.

He nodded eagerly. "Yes, *memsahib*. Very powerful man!"

"I'd like to see him," she said.

The boy looked upset. "This village is famous for

157

dancing," he trotted out. "We make very good drums. I show you?"

Arab agreed that she would like to see the drums. Everybody, it appeared, could play them in the village. Their four fingers and the ball of their palms became a blur as they beat out the intricate rhythms on the skins pulled tight over various hollowed-out pieces of wood.

"You try," the boy urged her.

She did so, but she wasn't very good at it. If she concentrated hard, she could beat out a simple melody, but the counter-beat was beyond her, and the giggles that her attempts to do better produced made her nervous.

"I want to see the witch-doctor," she repeated.

A woman who was nursing her baby nearby called out something to the boy at her side. "That is my mother," he told her. "She is one of the wives of the witch-doctor. She will take you to him."

The woman got to her feet with unconscious grace. She handed the baby over to his brother, rearranging the single sheet of material that she wore round her hips. When she smiled, Arab was astonished to see that she had perfect teeth and that her tongue darted in and out of her mouth every time she laughed, which was often. She beckoned to Arab to follow her, pausing every now and then to allow Arab to keep pace with her.

She led the way across the main compound of the village towards a hut that was a little larger than any of the others. With a gesture, she bade Arab wait outside while she drew back the curtain in the doorway and, ducking her head, entered into the gloomy interior.

Arab eased her foot into a more comfortable position, leaning heavily on the walking-stick. She felt quite sick with pain and her head ached. She hoped it was not a recurrence of malaria and put the thought away from her quickly in case it should be true. A goat came round the side of the hut and stood, stock-still, trying to make its mind up if she were an enemy to be butted or a friend to be ignored. Arab whistled to it through her teeth, hoping for the best, and the beast went slowly away, pausing only to take a mouthful of cloth that was hanging from a piece of string from another hut nearby.

Arab blinked at the sun and tried to move into the shade. The curtain twitched beside her and Hilary came rushing out.

"Arab! I'm so glad you came! I didn't see how you could! It was easy getting here, but I couldn't imagine how I was going to get home. But I got it! And he promises that it works—really it does! And it isn't poisonous, because I've tried a little of it myself and I'm still alive. It cost five whole shillings!"

Arab tripped over her walking-stick and fell heavily to the ground.

"What cost five shillings?"

Hilary flung herself on to her knees beside her, pulling the stick out from beneath her.

"The love potion!" she said.

CHAPTER ELEVEN

"A *love potion*?" Arab repeated. "Whatever for?"

Hilary helped her to her feet, frowning with concentration. "Mummy gave me the idea," she said. "You know, at breakfast this morning. I think it's a very good idea, don't you?"

Arab balanced herself with difficulty against the wall of the hut. If her jeans had been disreputable before, they were now in a very sad state indeed.

"It seems plain daft to me!" she said shortly.

"But it isn't, Arab!" Hilary looked hurt. "I got it for you," she explained. "I thought you'd stay with us for ever then."

"*Me*?" Arab stared at her, the pain in her foot temporarily forgotten. "For me?" The aggrieved expression on Hilary's face sharpened her temper. "Do you know how worried I've been, young lady? I've been half out of my mind all day, telling myself you were with Ayah, until I saw her and she told me she hadn't seen you all day either. You, Hilary, have some explaining to do! And a lot of guff about love potions isn't a very good beginning!"

Hilary went white. "I didn't think you'd worry," she said in a small voice.

"Of course I worried! Your mother and Lucien had gone out for the day, or they might have come looking for you. As it was, I couldn't even drive the car—"

"How did you get here?" Hilary asked.

"Jacques drove me." Arab was on the point of telling the child what a disaster that arrangement had been, when she realised that perhaps she had better not. "He's waiting in the Mini-Moke for us on the other side of the compound."

Hilary screwed up her face. "I think he might have

saved you having to walk all round the village!" she exclaimed. "I'm sorry, Arab, truly I am. I meant to find out what time the bus went back to Malindi, but it was going and I had to run to catch it, and then I didn't think of it again until we were nearly here."

Arab grunted. "You shouldn't go on buses by yourself!"

"I have to!" Hilary appealed. "I can't drive—*ever*!"

"You could have taken Ayah with you," Arab pointed out. "And what use is a love potion anyway?"

Hilary grinned, quick to see that Arab's curiosity was getting the better of her temper. "It was for you! You see, if you make Lucien some tea and put the potion in his cup, he'll love you for ever!"

"But—" Arab protested.

"For ever and ever," Hilary repeated. "The witch-doctor says so. Then you'll never have to go back to England, but you can stay here with us. It cost me five whole shillings, Arab, but I think it's worth it, don't you? It might not have worked," she went on thoughtfully, "if Aunt Sandra had been here, but with her away, *anything* might happen!"

"*Anything!*" Arab agreed with mounting exasperation. "But, Hilary, don't you see that you can't interfere like that? If Lucien loves Sandra, your love potion won't change it. People have to be allowed to make up their own minds about these things."

"Don't you love Lucien?"

Arab swallowed hard. "Yes," she admitted.

"Then why should Aunt Sandra have him? She doesn't love him! She doesn't love anyone!"

"Because Lucien loves *her*. He has the same right to feel as he does as you and I have."

Hilary looked appalled. "But then he won't ask you to marry him! That would be *awful*! When Mummy goes away, I always stay with Lucien, and I couldn't, I just couldn't, if Aunt Sandra were there too!"

"You may have to," Arab said.

"I won't!" The small girl stamped her foot. "I

161

won't! If you won't give Lucien the love potion, then I will! I won't have him marrying Aunt Sandra!"

Arab sighed, feeling quite as dejected as Hilary. "Come on," she said. "We have to get back to the airport to see them all off to Nairobi."

"I wish you hadn't come and found me! I don't want to see Aunt Sandra off!"

"What about Jill?" Arab reminded her.

"I don't mind Jill," the child agreed. "But she would understand. Have you seen Aunt Sandra and Mr. Silk talking together? He looks as though he's about to eat her up." She looked sulkily up at Arab. "And I don't like Jacques either!" she announced for good measure.

"Why ever not?" Arab gasped, chiding herself for encouraging Hilary to express these outrageous views.

Hilary shrugged. "He's never serious. I don't like people who say I'm going to be a peach when I grow up, and silly things like that! How does he know what I'll be like? I won't be in the least like a peach! I'm going to be clever and an anthropologist like Mummy, and he wouldn't like me at all because he isn't clever, is he? At least I don't think he is."

Devastated by the solemn air of candour with which this speech was delivered, Arab felt bound to try and defend him. "He's on holiday," she said. "He only wants a bit of fun!"

Hilary drew herself up to her full height. "Lucien doesn't like him!" she dismissed Jacques. "Lucien says he wishes he could put you in a veil, then you wouldn't attract so many undesirables to your side!" She giggled suddenly. "He must like you to say a thing like that. Don't you think?"

Arab refused to answer. The conceit of the man! "Hilary," she began uncertainly, "don't say anything about this love potion to anyone else. They might not understand—"

"I won't. It won't work if Lucien knows about it anyway. I might tell Mummy though. She'd be interested in whether it has the same ingredients as the ones in Ethiopia. You wouldn't mind my telling her, would you?"

Arab did mind, but she couldn't very well say so. She gritted her teeth and prepared for the walk back across the compound to the car. If Jacques had been in another mood she would have asked him to drive round the village to pick her up, but she knew that he wasn't inclined to indulge her and that there was nothing for it but to make her way somehow to him.

It took her a long time. Hilary walked slowly beside her, exchanging laughing remarks with half the village as they went. Arab herself felt too tired even to raise a smile for most of them. Her face was grey with pain and fatigue by the time they reached the car. Hilary fussed round her, trying to devise some easy way for her to get into the cockpit of the Mini-Moke, casting dark looks at Jacques at intervals who merely sat where he was, watching them.

"Jacques, we'll be late at the airport," Arab said at last a trifle desperately. "Please help me!"

"It will put the tariff up," he warned her.

"I don't care!" she retorted with total indifference. She had no intention of paying anyway. "Only please hurry! I haven't got time to change now as it is."

"I don't know that I care to have you in my car smelling like a goat," Jacques said, holding his nose with two fastidious fingers.

"Oh, shut up!" said Arab. "I'll manage without your help!"

She did so, but it cost her dear in effort and pain. Hilary helped her all she could, but she was not strong enough to take the burden of Arab's weight as she slung her good leg into the car. Hilary seized her plastered foot and lifted it with more enthusiasm than accuracy back on to its cushion.

"Are you all right, Arab?" she asked repeatedly. "You look awful!"

"Yes, doesn't she?" said Jacques.

"I know, I know. I wish I had time to change," Arab muttered ruefully. "Still, Jill won't care."

Jacques raised his eyebrows. "You are a funny girl to be a model," he said. "Sometimes you look gorgeous and golden, and now you look—"

"Like a street arab!" Hilary supplied with a little giggle. "That's what Lucien calls her. It's a pun on her name," she added in case Jacques had not seen it. "Lucien likes her jeans—"

"How do you know?" Arab asked quickly.

"You're wasting your time!" Jacques shot at her.

"I know," she admitted.

Hilary jumped into the back seat. "He does like them!" she claimed. "He said so! It was when Aunt Sandra said they were a disgrace and *he* said they were cute!"

Arab could feel herself blushing. "Do hurry up!" she commanded Jacques. "We're going to be late, I just know we are!"

They were. They were in sight of the airport when the Fokker Friendship aeroplane lifted into the sky and turned towards Nairobi. Arab watched it go in a stricken silence. Jill would know where she had gone and would understand, she thought, but the others would think that she hadn't been interested enough to come and wave them goodbye. They had been good to work with and she was sorry that they would think badly of her. It hurt. It hurt too that Lucien and Ruth would have been looking out for her when she hadn't been there.

"Never mind!" Hilary tried to comfort her, aware of Arab's deep disappointment. "You can write to Jill, or better still you can ring her up tonight. Lucien will get the number for you."

"Very cosy," Jacques put in. "But before that, *chérie*, there is the little matter of the payment you owe me."

Arab shrugged. "Not now, Jacques," she said. "I'm not in the mood."

"Are you ever? This was a gentleman's agreement,

ma mie. I thought the English always kept their word?"

"But it's ridiculous!" Arab protested. "I don't want to kiss you!"

"You should have thought of that before," he drawled.

"Why has she got to kiss you?" Hilary demanded, poised to jump out of the Mini-Moke. "I'm going to find Mummy and Lucien."

"*Bonne idée!*" said Jacques. "Bella and I will wait here. Yes, *ma belle?*"

It would be making too much of a foolish incident to ask Hilary to stay, Arab thought. If she had to kiss Jacques at all, she would kiss him quickly and have done.

"Very well," she said.

She was quite unprepared for the strength of his arms, or for the vicious way his mouth came down on hers. She attempted to get free of him, but she could not with the handicap that her foot presented. It was an uncomfortable experience, but she did nothing to help him. She no longer resisted him, but nor did she respond in any way to the warm pressure of his lips.

"You have a bad idea of paying your debts!" he grumbled against her throat.

"I didn't intend to pay at all!" she retorted.

"That was very obvious. You're not paying now in any way that counts. You could give me one good kiss—just to say goodbye, *non?*"

Arab smiled faintly. "*Oui,*" she said.

His arms closed about her again and this time she made some effort to respond to him, though he had no more effect on her than he had on the beach on the night of the dance. How different it had been with Lucien! She longed for the feel of Lucien's arms and the touch of his lips, but Jacques was nothing like Lucien and she felt only empty and dissatisfied. When at last he let her go, she put up a hand to wipe her lips and found herself looking straight into Lucien's furious eyes.

"We were too late for the plane," she said, her heart

pounding. The mere sight of him made her shrivel up with guilt. "I—I didn't even change."

"So I see," Lucien said in icy tones.

Jacques jumped out of the Mini-Moke, grinning. He put up a hand and slapped Lucien on the shoulder. "Jealous, *mon ami*?"

The contempt in Lucien's eyes scorched Arab to the bone, but had no effect on the Frenchman. Jacques merely laughed again.

"You are welcome to her," he said easily. "Bella is not at her most attractive this evening—a little difficult, shall we say? If you will help her out of my car, I will be getting back to the hotel."

Lucien said nothing. He put an arm about Arab and hooked her neatly out of the Moke, carrying her over to his own car where he deposited her, none too gently, on the front seat.

"I'm sorry," Arab said.

He didn't even look at her. "Jill damned nearly missed the plane herself! She went by the Villa Tanit expecting to find you there and waited for as long as she possibly could. Couldn't you have left a message, Arab?"

"I thought I'd be back in time—"

"What you mean is that you didn't think at all!" he snapped. "You preferred to go out with your French boy-friend and that was that!"

"It wasn't!" she protested.

"Then why did you go with him?"

A lump formed in the back of Arab's throat. "I—I—" she began in a tight, constricted voice.

"Don't bother!" Lucien advised nastily. "I saw the finale, remember? If you want someone to kiss you, my dear, I thought I'd made it clear that I'm both willing and available!"

"He was saying goodbye," Arab attempted to explain.

Lucien's head blocked off her view of the airport. That he was very angry she had no doubt whatsoever. She uttered a strangled gasp, but there was no way of escaping his kiss. But her own quick temper came to her rescue. She would *not* be kissed by Lucien because he despised her, or because he thought to punish her. How dared he treat her like that! She pulled back her hand and hit him as hard as she could across the face.

He drew back immediately, clasping both her hands in his. With a last desperate movement, she tried to get free of him, succeeded in freeing one hand and hit out at him again.

"Oh no, my dear!" he said in remarkably mild tones. "Once I'll allow you to get away with, but not twice!"

But Arab was beyond reason. She twisted her arm to one side and cast another wild blow at his head. But this time it was he who slapped her face and her face stung scarlet with the imprint of his hand.

"How dare you?" she cried furiously.

He smiled down at her, his own anger completely evaporated. "You asked for it, Arab. Now, suppose you calm down and tell me all about it?"

Arab chewed at her lower lip. "There's nothing to tell!" she denied.

His eyebrows shot up. "Nothing? D'you mean to tell me that affectionate scene was in aid of nothing?"

"I don't mean to tell you anything!" Arab shot back at him. "It's none of your business!"

"Okay, have it your own way. I have something to tell you. Jill is going to see your parents as soon as she can. I've sent a letter with her asking them to come out here for a visit. Do you think they'll come?"

Arab shook her head. "They'd love to," she said, "but they'd never be able to afford the fares. Anyway, they don't have to come. I'll be going back to England myself as soon as I can get a seat on a plane."

Lucien gave her a laconic smile. "There's no hurry. Wait and see how you feel about things when you get that plaster off your foot."

"I *can't* wait till then!"

"Why not?"

The colour surged into her cheeks. "I can't go on

staying with you for ever. It's—it's embarrassing to—to—"

He didn't answer her directly. He traced the mark that his hand had left on her cheek with his forefinger, smiling directly into her eyes. "We'll talk about it some other time," he said. "At the moment you look about ready for bed!"

Ruth, when she came out of the airport building with Hilary clutching at her hand, was the first to agree with him. She took one look at Arab and hurried her daughter into the back of the car.

"Dinner in bed for you!" she said firmly to Arab. "Ayah can help you out of those clothes the moment we get home. You were looking so much better too! Did you have to go tearing round the countryside in the heat of the afternoon?"

Hilary poked her mother in the ribs. "I was *telling* you," she began.

"Jacques has to go back to work soon," Arab broke in quickly. "I couldn't resist going for a jaunt with him in the Mini-Moke. I miss not being able to drive myself round. We were longer than we thought we'd be, though. I'm sorry to have missed Jill, but she'll understand."

"She wouldn't have approved of the romantic finish!" Lucien drawled. "I thought she'd warned you off that young man!"

Arab lifted her chin. "What if she did? I'm old enough to have my own friends. I'm quite capable of looking after myself!"

"It looked like it!" he taunted her.

Arab flushed. "He kisses very nicely," she claimed.

His sardonic eyes met hers. "My dear girl, I doubt you have enough experience to tell!"

"Lucien!" Ruth's outraged voice came from the rear. "That was unkind!"

"I don't feel kind!" he retorted.

"Well, don't take it out on my guest!" Ruth said sharply. She studied Arab's averted face with troubled eyes, noting the red mark on her cheek. "Even if you are jealous!" she added.

Lucien laughed shortly. "What did you have to say to Sandra that took so long?" he countered.

So that was who he was jealous of, Arab thought miserably. He had wanted to say goodbye to Sandra himself and when he hadn't been able to get her to himself, he had taken his temper out on her! Well, she didn't care! He could love whomever he liked and she wouldn't care at all!

"She is my sister-in-law," Ruth said mildly. "I wanted to make sure that she was happy about—things."

"And is she?" he demanded.

Ruth hesitated. "She isn't a happy sort of person," she hedged. "But I think this time she knows what she wants."

"That's the first step in the right direction," Lucien said. Arab studied him carefully to see what he was thinking, but he gave nothing away. His eyes met hers with a look of enquiry and she looked hastily away. She put her head back wearily and closed her eyes, longing for bed, and more than ever conscious of the tight knot in her stomach that only Lucien's touch could assuage.

It was only a few minutes' drive back to the Villa Tanit. Hilary chatted happily all the way, making it unnecessary for her elders to say anything at all. She had particularly noticed a whole lot of new people who had flown in from Nairobi and she wanted to know all about them.

"Don't you know any of them?" she asked her mother.

"One or two of them," Ruth answered her. "I was talking to them when you came in to fetch me."

"You didn't introduce me!" Hilary complained.

"No," her mother agreed. "I was afraid that smell of goat was coming from you."

Hilary chuckled. "It was," she admitted without resentment. "Arab smells even worse!"

Lucien made a play of twitching his nose in Arab's

direction. "So she does!" He glanced at her and back to the road ahead. "So you had a chaperone after all!"

"Some of the time," Arab said.

"But you're still not going to tell me about it?"

Arab smiled, "No."

She could almost hear Hilary's breath of relief and wondered if Lucien had too. Silly child, she thought. She would have them all asking questions if she looked so guilty!

But there was no time for more questions just then. Lucien parked the car outside the front door and, without waiting to be asked, lifted Arab into his arms and marched into the house and up the stairs, putting her down gently on her bed. She opened her mouth to thank him, but he was already gone, shouting for Ayah as he went.

Ayah came running. Her large, gentle hands eased Arab's clothes off her aching body.

"You having a shower, *memsahib*?"

Arab grinned at her. "I suppose so. I shall have to get rid of the goat smell somehow."

Ayah shook her head. "That be Memsahib Kjana! You find her all right? I tell her something when I get her alone!"

"No, don't!" Arab pleaded for the child. "She thought she was doing me a favour. I think she's going to tell her mother all about it."

Ayah looked extremely uncertain. "But I get into bad trouble! She very naughty girl!"

Arab stepped under the shower, rejoicing in the feel of the cool water on her hot, prickly flesh. It was a bit awkward because she had to try and keep the plaster dry by sticking her foot out at an angle, but anything was worth the sheer bliss of the water running over her. She was just about to step out again, taking care not to slip on the wet floor, when Ayah advanced towards her, a shampoo in one hand, and set about washing her hair with an energy that left Arab as limp as a worn-out rag.

"Surely I don't smell as badly as that!" she objected in muffled tones as her head was seized and pushed firmly under the shower.

"No, it ain't that you smell bad, but I have the shampoo right here!" Ayah responded, with all the confidence of the universal nanny. "You feel better when you good and clean."

The funny thing was that she did. She sat up in bed with her pillows fluffed up behind her and hoped that somebody would remember to bring her some food. She was *starving*! It was quite indecent for anyone to be as miserable as she was and yet be hungry, but she couldn't help it. She kept looking at her watch, trying to make the time go faster, but the hands crawled round until at last it was nearly eight o'clock and she knew that supper had to be soon.

A faint knock at the door brought a quick "*Karibu*" from her. Ruth pushed open the door and advanced a few steps into the room.

"You weren't asleep, were you?"

Arab looked up eagerly. "No, of course not." She smiled sheepishly. "To tell you the truth I was hoping that someone was going to bring me some food."

Ruth chuckled. "I have. I left it on the landing while I made sure that you were ready to receive it. We've already had ours, but I thought I'd come up for a while and talk to you while you have yours." She went out again and came back with a heavily-laden tray. "I'm glad to hear you're hungry," she went on approvingly. "I thought my little daughter had reduced you to a frazzle."

"I must be resilient," Arab smiled.

"You need to be with Hilary around. Arab, I don't believe in apologising for other people, not even one's children, but I've had the whole story from Hilary and I'd like you to believe that she didn't mean any harm."

Arab blushed, glad that she could hide behind her dinner tray. "I was rather touched," she said gruffly.

Ruth's sharp eyes rested for an instant on the younger girl's face. "If I were another kind of mother, I think I'd be quite jealous of the friendship between you and Hilary." Her eyes danced as they met Arab's astonished gaze. "Oh, it's all right, I'm not! Only it has made me think. My work takes me to the back of beyond quite a lot and I don't really like leaving Hilary, though there's no problem all the time she can stay with Lucien. What I hadn't realised was how much it worried her that Lucien might marry someone she didn't like." She broke off, shrugging her shoulders.

"Sandra," Arab put in dryly.

Ruth smiled. "Yes. Sandra." She was silent for a long moment. "I don't know how Lucien feels about Sandra," she said at last. "But I do know my sister-in-law. She's a few years older than Lucien and she certainly wouldn't want to be reminded of that—ever! So I asked her what she did intend to do with her life." She was quiet again, staring thoughtfully at Arab's plate. "I thought I'd tell you what she said, but I don't want to seem like an interfering busybody. She says she plans to be the next Mrs. Sammy Silk!"

"No!" gasped Arab.

Ruth nodded slowly. "I knew she had a yen that way, but I had to be sure. It was odd, and rather sad, to see Sandra sizing up her chances with real humility. Sammy, it seems, is an unknown quantity."

Arab felt suddenly quite gay. "Jill says he's dotty about her!" she said with satisfaction.

Ruth looked amused. "What a pity we couldn't try out Hilary's potion on him!" she joked. "It might have worked!"

Arab sniffed. "Unlikely!" she opined.

"You're good with Hilary," Ruth said suddenly. "She actually understood what you said about Lucien having to make his own choice, though I'm afraid she still feels a little push in the right direction would help matters along. She asked me to give you the love potion, just in case you had second thoughts about it! She'd have come herself, but she has been put to bed by an irate Ayah."

Arab accepted the small package, opening it immediately because her curiosity was thoroughly aroused as to what the mixture could consist of. She smelt it cautiously and was revolted.

"Goodness!" she said. "It's powerful stuff!"

"I think Hilary would expect something pretty powerful for five shillings!" Ruth remarked with a laugh.

"It's disgusting!" Arab announced. "Have a sniff?"

Ruth made a face at the powder. "I hope you're not going to use it," she said. "I'm rather fond of my brother, and I prefer to have him alive!"

Arab's hands shook. She put the potion down on her bedside table before Ruth should notice. "I don't seem to be quite as hungry as I thought I was," she said. "It's been a long day!"

But Ruth was not so easily diverted. "Shall I send Lucien up to say goodnight?" she asked, as she reached for Arab's tray.

"*No!*" Arab blenched. "No," she said more normally. "Ayah insisted on washing my hair and I feel like a half-drowned rat still. Besides—"

Ruth looked enquiringly at her.

"I don't want him to feel responsible for me. He carries on as if I had no mind of my own. He treats me as if I were Hilary's age!" She heaved a sigh. "Sometimes I wish I were!" she added.

Ruth smiled at her affectionately. "Lucien is more observant than you suppose," she said. "But I understand, love. He's a bossy brute where all his womenfolk are concerned, only Hilary and I seem to like it!" She went towards the door. "Goodnight, Arab, and thanks for rescuing my offspring."

"Think nothing of it," Arab answered. "Goodnight."

She lay quite still for a long time after Ruth had gone, watching a moth that was flying round her bedside light intent on suicide. It made a flicking noise every time it hit the shade, but it still came back to the light.

Supposing, she thought, that Sandra did marry Sammy Silk. And supposing that Lucien found that he didn't mind as much as he had thought he would. Supposing, just supposing, that he turned to her with marriage in mind, she would fly into his arms and nothing would stop her.

She turned her thoughts away from Lucien, settling herself down to sleep with determination, but she had never felt less sleepy. Then she sat up straight with a bang, knocking her book off the bed on to the floor. Why had Lucien written to her parents? And why had he wanted them to meet his family? She lay down again, shivering with an unexpected and unknown excitement. She had to sleep because she couldn't wait for tomorrow to come, tomorrow and Lucien.

CHAPTER TWELVE

BUT in the morning Ruth insisted that Arab should have her breakfast in bed and it was nearly lunchtime when she finally got dressed and went downstairs, clutching on to the banisters in lieu of a crutch. Having gained the sitting room, she sank into the nearest chair, listening to the voices of Hilary and Lucien as they floated in to her from the garden. After a few minutes though she had caught her breath and she went outside to join them in the shade of the trees.

Hilary danced over to her immediately. "You can have my chair," she offered. "I don't want to sit down any more."

Arab thanked her demurely. She had dressed with enormous care, choosing a light green dress with puritan collar and cuffs. In it she looked cool and fresh, and anyway, it made a change from her jeans. But as soon as she met Lucien's mocking gaze, she knew exactly why she had chosen that particular dress and, worse, she knew that he knew it too. It was a dress which stressed her feminine appeal and left no doubt that she was a fully-grown woman.

Hilary draped herself over the back of Arab's chair. "Did Mummy give it to you? Have you used it yet? Have you, Arab?"

"No. I told you, I'm not going to!"

Hilary looked sulky. "I thought you might. The coffee tasted funny at breakfast time and I thought—"

Arab laughed. "That I'd been creeping round the house at crack of dawn—with *this*?" She pointed to her broken ankle. "It takes me a good ten minutes to get downstairs, I'll have you know!"

Hilary sighed. "I'd do it for you, but it might not work then." She thought for a moment. "It's your birthday present, you know, because I can't afford to get you anything else, so I do think you might use it!"

Lucien smiled across at his niece. "What present is this?"

Hilary instantly became more cautious. "It's a secret," she said, "between Arab and me."

Lucien's amused gaze swung on to Arab's face. "I see," he drawled. "I suppose you bought it yesterday?"

"Yes, of course," Hilary nodded. "I went on the bus." Arab cast her a quick look of warning, but the child paid no attention to her. "I like going on the bus."

"How did you get home?" Lucien asked.

Hilary licked her lips. "Mummy knows all about it," she said.

Arab stirred restively under Lucien's interested gaze. "Will—will you drive me to the airport some time?" she asked him. "I want to enquire about when I can get home to England."

"No, I won't!" he said shortly. "Well, Hilary?"

The child capitulated. "Arab came and got me," she admitted.

"Before lunch?"

Hilary shook her head. "There wasn't a bus coming the other way," she explained. "I didn't know what to do, though they were all very kind and nice and one of the witchdoctor's wives gave me a sweet potato to eat."

Lucien didn't look at all angry. "Didn't you get any lunch?" he enquired sympathetically.

"No. I didn't get any tea either, because Arab insisted that we rushed to the airport, and then Jacques was being silly and he made her kiss him because he'd driven her round looking for me—"

"Really?" Lucien drawled. "Why didn't you get Jill to drive you?" he demanded of Arab.

Her face flamed. "Jill doesn't drive," she answered uncomfortably. If she had been normally fleet of foot, she would have run away then, leaving Hilary to face her uncle on her own. But her foot tied her to her seat and the only weapon that was left to her was her tongue. "As Hilary said, your sister knows all about it, so I don't see that it's any business of yours!" she declared.

Lucien merely grinned. "I'm making it my business. I'm very interested in this French boy-friend of yours. I thought you were old enough to deal with him?" he added slyly.

"I am!"

"It doesn't look much like it! *When* are you twenty-one?"

"You know perfectly well!" Arab snapped. "If you won't drive me to the airport, I'll ask Ruth if she will. I intend to spend my birthday in England!" She very nearly added 'so there!', but the last thing she wanted was to give him an opening so that he could accuse her of childishness, so she restrained herself, contenting herself with glaring at him with as much dignity as she could manage under the circumstances.

Lucien got leisurely to his feet. He came over to Arab, imprisoning her by leaning a hand on either arm of her chair.

"When you're twenty-one—" he began.

"I'll be in England!" she said faintly.

"No, my darling little street arab, you'll be here with me, whatever you like to think." He ducked his head and kissed her briefly on the mouth. "Well?"

Arab heard Hilary's happy chuckle beside her and her heart missed a beat. "When I'm twenty-one I still won't have an affair with you!" she said desperately.

He laughed. "Don't be too sure of that!" he whispered, and he kissed her again, a fleeting, tantalising kiss that made her want him more than ever.

"I'm quite sure," she replied.

"Such confidence!" he teased her. "Will you be so cool and sure of yourself when I take you to see the Giriama dancers tonight?"

"T—tonight?"

He stood up straight, ruffling her hair as he did so.

"Tonight," he said solemnly. "You're near enough to twenty-one!"

It was inevitable that Hilary wanted to go too. She did everything she could to persuade her uncle, even offering to tell him what her present to Arab had been, but he would not be moved.

"I think you're mean!" she told him at the lunch table.

Lucien made a face at her. "This is something you've gone to a lot of trouble to help along," he smiled. "Why try and spoil it now?"

Hilary gave him a puzzled look. "But I don't want you to go by yourselves!" she objected. "Why can't Mummy and I come?"

Lucien laughed out loud. "Because I'm going to steal your present and turn the tables on Arab!"

Hilary's eyes widened. "You know what it is!" she accused him.

"It won't work for you," Arab assured him blithely, not knowing whether it would or not. "And I wouldn't *stoop* so low—"

"Only because you don't have to!" he retorted, amused by this display of spirit. "You use a different alchemy, like a pretty dress and a new lipstick."

"I haven't got a new lipstick!" Arab denied, but she blushed all the same, remembering how Hilary had told her the first time they had met, that Lucien didn't like women to wear trousers! It was an uncomfortable thought, that he knew she had worn this particular dress for him.

Hilary, who had been silent during this exchange, gave a sudden whoop of laughter. "I don't mind not coming after all!" she announced. "Mummy and I can go some other time."

"Oh, but—" Arab objected. "*But*—"

Ruth's eyes twinkled with amusement. "I really believe my daughter is learning a little tact," she observed. "You're surely not going to spoil it, Arab?"

"I—"

"Arab will do as she's told," Lucien cut in. "Methinks she protests too much anyway!"

"And I think you're quite *beastly*!" Arab told him, temper coming to the aid of her stuttering tongue.

His eyebrows shot up. "Do you now?" he drawled. "Hasn't anyone ever told you, my love, that a spoonful of honey catches more flies than a whole barrel of vinegar?"

"Who wants to catch flies?" she retorted.

Hilary gurgled with laughter. "He means himself!" she explained to Arab. "Don't you want to catch him?"

"No, I do not! Why should I want to? All he ever does is make personal remarks and work me to death! It will be a holiday, being back in England. My mother will nurse me back to my usual rude health, giving me my breakfast in bed—"

"You had breakfast in bed today!" Hilary interrupted, frowning.

"And my friends will all be glad to see me," Arab went on breathlessly, not daring to stop. "They don't care *what* I wear! And they all agree that my hair is auburn. They even respect my opinions about—things!"

"What things?" Lucien taunted.

Ruth gave them both a confused look. "But isn't your hair auburn?" she asked Arab.

"Of course it is!" Arab declared. "Only your daughter says it isn't red enough to be auburn, while your brother—" She cast him a look of burning indignation— "says it's dull copper!"

"To match your temper," he added lazily. "You've forgotten that bit!"

"I have not!" She broke off, hotly embarrassed that she had revealed how well she remembered every word he had said to her. "It isn't in the least bit funny!" she went on in the face of Ruth's laughter. "I want to go home!"

Lucien's eyes filled with amusement. "Do you?" he mocked. "What about my notes that you haven't finished yet?"

"There you are!" Arab declared triumphantly. "I knew you only wanted me here because I can type!"

"It'll give you something to do this afternoon," Lucien agreed promptly. "It will keep you from missing me while I'm away."

"Away?" she repeated, fighting the tide of dismay that rose within her and which she knew was, humiliatingly, reflected on her face.

Laughter danced in his eyes. "I have to get the tickets for tonight—and something else. Can you bear it?"

Arab lifted her head and looked him straight in the face. "Easily!" she boasted.

In fact the afternoon passed slowly. She worked on Lucien's notes and was intrigued to discover that the Assyrian horn of power had had the same significance amongst the first rulers of the East African coast. There was an ivory horn extant in Lamu, and one in Zanzibar that had belonged to the African ruler, long before the coming of the Arab Sultan. It was strange to think of the various strands that had gone to make up the ancient trading world, and which ones existed now, while others had long since fallen into decay.

But even her interest in Lucien's work was dulled by the long wait for the evening to come. The pile of neatly-typed sheets of paper grew at her elbow, but her heart was not in it. Not even a reference to Cheng Ho could rouse her from the feeling of sheer panic she had every time she thought of Lucien.

A lilac-breasted roller came into the garden at tea time and had a dust bath close to where she was working, its green back fluffed up, almost hiding the fantastic shades of blue and mauve of its breast. Then she moved her foot by accident and the bird flew away, its round, black eye suspicious of her and the clacking typewriter in front of her. The incident brought home to her how much there was of beauty in Africa. Not only the birds, but the gay, flowering shrubs, and the bright cannas in the flower beds. It would be hard to be satisfied with the more muted colours of an English garden after this, even if she were lucky enough to ever have one.

But the sun eventually faded from the sky, the scarlet, gold and vivid green of sunset giving way to the velvet blackness of the night, and Ruth came out to help her in with the typewriter and Lucien's notes.

"You've just got time to have a drink before changing for dinner," she announced. "Do you want a hand, or can you manage?"

"I can manage, thank you," Arab assured her. Despite the length of the afternoon, she still wanted time to think which dress she was going to wear, and whether she should put her hair up to make herself look older, or leave it hanging down her back as she usually did.

Ayah came in to help her dress. "You lookin' pretty, *memsahib*!" she exclaimed as she wound a stole about Arab's shoulders. "As pretty as I seen you! Bwana Lucien very lucky man!"

Arab looked at herself in the glass, carefully applying some eye-shadow and just the right amount of powder to hide the freckles on her nose.

"I hope so," she said. "I almost wish Sandra hadn't gone to England, though. Do you think he would be taking me to see the Giriama dancing if she had been here?"

Ayah rolled her eyes and giggled, her massive body shaking up and down. "You jokin', *memsahib*?"

Arab shook her head. She thought she looked pale despite her make-up, but it was too hot to wear anything greasy.

"You not jokin'? Don't you know that the Bwana told her to go away. He say to her that she do your job very well and why don't she try it. He don't want her hanging round the house. He tell her flat! He even tell her to use your seat on the aeroplane. You stayin' right here with him, he say! Don't you know that?"

"No, I didn't know," Arab said.

"And he send for Memsahib Ruth," Ayah continued, well away now she had got started. "He send for her to come right home at once because he met you and want you to stay!"

"But she didn't say anything about it to me!" Arab protested.

"Why else you think she come?" Ayah demanded belligerently. "She come quick!" She threw back her head and roared with delighted laughter. "Ayah knows! Ayah hears many things!"

That Arab could believe! She glanced at the large African woman in the glass, smiling mischievously, while she screwed her ear-rings into her ears. When she had done, she stood up and hugged the massive woman in a sudden excess of joy.

"Will you help me down the stairs?" she said.

Lucien was waiting for her in the hall. He was wearing his jade green dinner jacket and was as handsome as he had ever looked. He was holding a pair of crutches in his hands and he smiled up at her as she slowly descended the stairs.

"I thought these might make you more mobile," he said. "You can try them out this evening, as long as you don't use them to run away from me!"

"Why should I?" she retorted, her head erect. "I'm not afraid of you!"

"No?" he grinned.

She blushed a little. "You do have a heavy hand," she admitted. "But I have almost forgiven you for that!"

They laughed together. Lucien handed the crutches to Ayah, sweeping Arab up into his arms and out of the house into his car. Before letting her go, he kissed her gently on the cheek where he had slapped her. "I shan't beat you tonight," he whispered. "That's a promise!"

"I should hope so!" she said bravely. She wished he didn't have to take his arms away because she felt lonely without the comfort of his touch. "Is it far to the village?" she asked him.

"About ten miles." He stowed the crutches away in

the back of the car and climbed in beside her. "You're looking very pretty tonight, Arab."

"And quite, quite grown up?"

"Yes, my rare, long-legged bird, quite grown up."

"Well, that's a relief!" she murmured, smiling at her own impertinence. "I was beginning to think that you'd never believe it!"

She could see his grin in the silver light from the moon. "Is that what you were trying to prove? I thought you'd decided you could do very well without me?"

"No," she said. "I said I didn't want to have an affair with you."

His knuckles shone white against the wheel. "That's too bad! Because I want to have a life-long affair with you, and I'm accustomed to getting my own way."

She trembled inwardly. "With *me*? Are you sure?"

He nodded briefly. "Darling, I'm ashamed to admit that for a while I didn't have marriage in mind. I've always thought it wouldn't be fair to any woman to tie her up to someone like me. I liked my freedom to take off to the farthest part of the world whenever the fancy took me. I'm in love with my work, and I never thought to find a woman who would understand that love. Then, if I had a wife, I would want children, and children can't be shuffled round the world like suitcases. But if we take Hilary for Ruth, she can look after our lot at other times—"

Arab stared into the darkness. She had never thought about children of her own, children with dark, arrogant features like Lucien's! *Their children*!

"I suppose you've discussed it all with Ruth?" she murmured.

"I had to tell her something. It took some doing to get her to fly back from Ethiopia! But I knew you wouldn't stay unless I did something! And I couldn't trust myself not to do something desperate if I had you to myself. You've tried me pretty highly, Arabella Burnett! Flirting with Sammy Silk and kissing Jacques Bouyer, and managing to look as innocent and young as Hilary, while all the time I wanted to do much more to you than just kiss you!"

Arab swallowed hard. "I—I thought you wanted a brief encounter—"

"What else could I say?" he demanded. "You were here for exactly three weeks! And you're so desperately young! It seemed little better than kidnap to rush you into marriage before you had time to look round. I'd have gone mad if you hadn't broken your ankle! When I kissed you in the House of the Scissors, I knew I couldn't let you go—"

"But you were going to all the same!" she exclaimed bitterly.

"That's all you know, my pet. It was then that I thought of Sandra!"

"I thought you were in love with her," Arab told him shyly. "In a way," she amended. "I thought you'd decided to marry her anyway. She thought so too."

"Sandra never thought anything of the kind!" he said so firmly that she had to believe him. "She has a great sense of the dramatic and she can't resist striking attitudes. It may have appealed to her that Ruth should marry her brother and she should marry me, but she would have loathed being my wife, just as she loathed my work and everything to do with it. I daresay Mr. Silk will suit her very well."

Arab threaded her fingers together with a fierce concentration. "Don't you mind—even a little bit—that she wants to marry Sammy?"

He brought the car to a stop and turned to face her with an air of triumph. "Jealous, Arab?" he asked her.

She thought of pretending that she was nothing of the kind, but she abandoned the idea at once. "Of course I'm jealous," she said instead. "I've been unbearably jealous of her ever since that first afternoon, when she walked into your sitting room as though she owned it!"

He laughed delightedly. "I thought you disliked me! I thought so even more when you declared that I liked my women to be sycophants! That was a cruel thrust!"

"Did I?" She could not remember doing so. She sighed. "I wanted to make such an impression on you and I felt such a fool. I wish I had one half of your confidence!"

"Sandra isn't so bad," he said. "She was quite agreeable to trying to do you out of a job—"

"Very kind of her!" Arab said dryly.

Lucien laughed again. "It didn't matter once you had broken your ankle, but if you hadn't, darling, there was no other hope of keeping you here!"

Arab gave him an indignant look. "I'm surprised you didn't make sure that I did break something! Perhaps you did! Perhaps you deliberately tripped me up!"

"I didn't think of it," he said slowly, "or I might have done."

"I knew it! You had it all arranged! You won't allow me a say in anything—"

He reached out for her, drawing her close against him. "Absolutely nothing!" he agreed smugly. "Be still! I want to kiss you!"

She went into his arms with an eagerness that shocked her. He held her close, not hurrying her at all, but finally his mouth found hers and, with a little sob of delight, her arms went up behind his neck and she gave herself up to the warmth and excitement of his embrace.

"Love me?" he asked at last, pulling gently at her hair.

"You know I do," she said. "Do you love me?"

"More than I thought it possible to love any woman! I hope your parents come quickly, my sweet, for I don't fancy waiting long for you!"

She smiled, completely happy. "You won't have to!" she said.

They had dinner at the hotel. Arab strove to reduce some sort of order to her appearance before they reached the lights of the reception room, but Lucien only laughed at her and ran his fingers through her hair all over again.

"You look as though you've been kissed!" he mocked her as he held the door for her to enter.

"I ought to care," she answered, "but I want the whole world to know that you've chosen me." Her eyes were soft as they peeked up at him. "I can still hardly believe it myself."

"You need a lot of convincing!" he teased her.

"But not right now!" she exclaimed, side-stepping round him hastily with crutches slipping dangerously on the marble floor.

He grinned. "It will be dark at the Giriama village, I'll see what I can do about convincing you then!"

"Beast!" she murmured.

It was a wonderful experience to be wined and dined by Lucien. There was no one she knew in the dining room and she supposed that Jacques and Jean-Pierre had gone back to their rocket project. She was glad that there was no one there but themselves, for Lucien was in a sparkling mood and she had to give all her attention to parrying his thrusts. Her happiness was still too new for her not to feel shy with him, but she was aware of a new gentleness, almost tenderness, she had never suspected he possessed, and the knowledge that he was as vulnerable as she, sent little waves of sheer bliss racing round her veins. Watching him across the table, she could no longer doubt that he loved her.

Arab had no idea what she ate, any more than she had any idea of which way Lucien drove to get to the village. She loved the velvety softness of the night, with its strange, tropical smells and sounds. She saw the sea briefly, unmistakable for its inky blackness edged with the white of the waves breaking against the shore. But then they went inland, the trees grew high all round them and, she thought, mysterious in the darkness.

The clearing in the village was lit by hurricane lamps hung around the huts and from the trees. Some wooden forms had been placed round in a rough semi-circle, and a few Europeans were already seated on them having been brought there from the various hotels round about. On the other side of the circle, the villagers sat in groups, the women to one side and the men on the other. Lucien told Arab that most of the women would have danced themselves before they married and that they provided the most critical part of the audience. The men were mostly young, pretending an indifference to everything that went on, although it was here at the dance that most of them took the first steps towards choosing a bride.

The girls themselves were very young. The smallest came on first, walking their way through a simple number while their proud parents beat the rhythm out for them on the drums.

Lucien put his arm round Arab and drew her back against his shoulder. "Tired, darling?" he asked her.

She shook her head. "Just happy," she said.

He pulled her closer still, saying something in Swahili to an old man standing nearby. The old man laughed and went off into the darkness beneath the trees.

"What did you say to him?" Arab murmured.

He chuckled and kissed her ear. "It would only embarrass you if I told you," he teased her. "Isn't it enough that I prefer you to all this bevy of beauty?"

She was glad of the darkness that covered her blushes. "Do we have to stay to the end?" she asked.

His eyes were dark pools of black, but she knew that if she had been able to see them they would have been full of mocking amusement. "No," he said. "We'll see the comedy turn and then we'll go."

The story was very simple, no more than a young wife of an old man who took a lover and came to regret her infidelity. But the acting was exuberant, especially from the young man who took the part of the lover, who seduced the young bride with love and with charm. Lucien took a tighter hold of Arab and she turned her face up to his, knowing that he was wanting to kiss her. She put her hand up under his jacket, delighting in the hard feel of his back. When the kiss came to an end, she was shaking.

"Come on," he said. "We're going now!"

She didn't dare argue with him. She, too, was beginning to hope that her parents came soon, before she cast all discretion to the wind and gave herself up completely to Lucien's lovemaking.

"How long is Ruth staying?" she asked, to give herself something else to think about.

"I think she'd better stay until we're properly wed," he answered, unconsciously echoing her own thoughts. He lifted her into his arms, sending her crutches crashing to the ground. "Come on, my love," he said. "We're going home!"

Arab wouldn't let him help her out of the car. She balanced the crutches that someone had retrieved for her at the village, and swung herself along between them, knowing that if she allowed him to kiss her again she wouldn't be able to stop. It was like trying to force the water back up a waterfall, such was the strength of her feeling for him.

"You won't ever leave me behind when you go off, will you?" she said in the doorway, suddenly anxious.

"Not if I can help it! Who would type my notes?"

"Because I don't think I could bear it!" Arab gulped.

Lucien came into the light. "Do you think I could?" he demanded. He smiled sweetly at her. "That reminds me that I have a present for you, though. We'll have to have a home somewhere and I thought it might as well be here." He put a hand in his breast pocket and drew out an official-looking document, looking ashamed of himself and as if he were afraid she was going to reject his gift. "I've bought you this house as a wedding present," he said.

She pushed the crutches away from her and fell into his arms. "Were you so sure of me?" she asked softly.

"I thought the house might help my case along," he answered. "Oh, darling, I wanted you so badly!"

"And I you!" she whispered back, and kissed him eagerly on the lips.

A sound on the stairs made them turn their heads towards the light of the hall. Hilary came bounding down the stairs, her dressing gown trailing behind her.

"Did you ask her? Did you?" She rushed across the hall to Arab. "Are you going to marry him?"

Arab coloured finely. "Yes, I am," she said happily.

Hilary hugged her. "I hope you're grateful," she said to her uncle. "Arab is *my* friend because I found her!"

Lucien smiled at her, taking the child's hand in his. "I'm very grateful," he told her. He looked up and saw his sister coming down the stairs too. "I'm grateful to your mother too," he went on. "But I'd be more grateful still if you'd all go back to bed!"

His womenfolk faced him in a united group of three. "Yes, Lucien," they said meekly, and they went up the stairs together, with Arab only a little slower than the other two.

16 GREAT RE-ISSUES

Here is a wonderful opportunity to read many of the Harlequin Romances you may have missed.

- ☐ 917 TIMBER MAN
  Joyce Dingwell
- ☐ 920 MAN AT MULERA
  Kathryn Blair
- ☐ 926 MOUNTAIN MAGIC
  Susan Barrie
- ☐ 944 WHISPER OF DOUBT
  Andrea Blake
- ☐ 973 TIME OF GRACE
  Sara Seale
- ☐ 976 FLAMINGOS ON THE LAKE
  Isobel Chace
- ☐ 980 A SONG BEGINS
  Mary Burchell
- ☐ 992 SNARE THE WILD HEART
  Elizabeth Hoy
- ☐ 996 PERCHANCE TO MARY
  Celine Conway
- ☐ 997 CASTLE THUNDERBIRD
  Susan Barrie
- ☐ 999 GREEN FINGERS FARM
  Joyce Dingwell
- ☐ 1014 HOUSE OF LORRAINE
  Rachel Lindsey
- ☐ 1027 THE LONELY SHORE
  Anne Weale
- ☐ 1223 THE GARDEN OF PERSEPHO
  Nan Asquith
- ☐ 1245 THE BAY OF MOONLIGHT
  Rose Burghley
- ☐ 1319 BRITTLE BONDAGE
  Rosalind Brett

To: HARLEQUIN READER SERVICE, Dept. N 401
M.P.O. Box 707, Niagara Falls, N.Y. 14302
Canadian address: Stratford, Ont., Canada

☐ Please send me the free Harlequin Romance Catalogue.
☐ Please send me the titles checked.

I enclose $_____ (No C.O.D.'s). All books are 60c each. To help defray postage and handling cost, please add 25c.

Name _____

Address _____

City/Town _____

State/Prov. _____ Zip _____

FREE! Harlequin Romance Catalogue

Here is a wonderful opportunity to read many of the Harlequin Romances you may have missed.

The HARLEQUIN ROMANCE CATALOGUE lists hundreds of titles which possibly are no longer available at your local bookseller. To receive your copy, just fill out the coupon below, mail it to us, and we'll rush your catalogue to you!

Following this page you'll find a sampling of a few of the Harlequin Romances listed in the catalogue. Should you wish to order any of these immediately, kindly check the titles desired and mail with coupon.

To: HARLEQUIN READER SERVICE, Dept. N 401
M.P.O. Box 707, Niagara Falls, N.Y. 14302
Canadian address: Stratford, Ont., Canada

☐ Please send me the free Harlequin Romance Catalogue.
☐ Please send me the titles checked.

I enclose $ _____ (No C.O.D.'s), All books are 60c each. To help defray postage and handling cost, please add 25c.

Name _____

Address _____

City/Town _____

State/Prov. _____ Zip _____

N 401

Have You Missed Any of These Harlequin Romances?

- [ ] 463 NURSE BRODIE Kate Norway
- [ ] 472 YOUNG DOCTOR KIRKDENE
      Elizabeth Hoy
- [ ] 492 HOSPITAL PRO
      Marjorie Moore
- [ ] 498 NURSE ATHOLL RETURNS
      Jane Arbor
- [ ] 712 HOUSE OF CONFLICT
      Mary Burchell
- [ ] 723 FORTUNE GOES BEGGING
      Margaret Malcolm
- [ ] 788 THE GENTLE SURGEON
      Hilda Pressley
- [ ] 923 KIT CAVENDISH — PRIVATE NURSE Margaret Malcolm
- [ ] 939 DOCTOR'S DAUGHTER
      Jean S. Macleod
- [ ] 951 THE ENCHANTED TRAP
      Kate Starr
- [ ] 953 ALEX RAYNER, DENTAL NURSE Marjorie Lewty
- [ ] 955 NURSE WITH A PROBLEM
      Jane Marnay
- [ ] 957 NO LEGACY FOR LINDSAY
      Essie Summers
- [ ] 959 WHO LOVES BELIEVES
      Elizabeth Hoy
- [ ] 961 NURSE JANE AND COUSIN PAUL Valerie K. Nelson
- [ ] 963 NURSE WILLOW'S WARD
      Jan Tempest
- [ ] 968 SWEET BRENDA
      Penelope Walsh
- [ ] 970 A CHALLENGE TO NURSE HONOR Pauline Ash
- [ ] 986 SURGEON AT WITTERINGHAM
      Hilda Nickson
- [ ] 993 SEND FOR NURSE ALISON
      Marjorie Norrell
- [ ] 995 NURSE RONNIE'S VOCATION
      Felicity Hayle
- [ ] 1002 A DOCTOR FOR DIANA
       Margaret Malcolm
- [ ] 1009 NURSE AT FAIRCHILDS
       Marjorie Norrell
- [ ] 1011 THE TURQUOISE SEA
       Hilary Wilde
- [ ] 1016 TWO PATHS Jean S. Macleod
- [ ] 1019 FLOWER OF THE MORNING
       Celine Conway
- [ ] 1022 YOUNG ELLIS
       Margery Hilton
- [ ] 1033 WITH LOVE FROM DR LUCIEN
       Pauline Ash
- [ ] 1041 NURSE AVERIL'S WARD
       Mary Hunton
- [ ] 1049 THE YOUNGEST NIGHT NURSE
       Anne Durham
- [ ] 1058 NURSE AT ROWANBANK
       Flora Kidd
- [ ] 1062 ONE SUMMER'S DAY
       Catherine Airlie
- [ ] 1074 NEW SURGEON AT ST. LUCIAN'S
       Elizabeth Houghton
- [ ] 1081 NURSE JANE IN TENERIFFE
       Catherine Airlie
- [ ] 1090 NURSE KATE AT FALLOWFIELD Ivy Ferrari
- [ ] 1113 BEQUEST FOR NURSE BARBARA Pauline Ash
- [ ] 1118 LAMENT FOR LOVE
       Jean S. Macleod
- [ ] 1141 THE VALLEY OF DESIRE
       Catherine Airlie
- [ ] 1144 THE TRUANT BRIDE
       Sara Seale
- [ ] 1188 THE GROTTO OF JADE
       Margery Hilton
- [ ] 1225 NURSE CAMDEN'S CAVALIER
       Louise Ellis
- [ ] 1240 THE GREEN RUSHES
       Catherine Airlie
- [ ] 1260 WE LIVE IN SECRET
       Dorothy Rivers
- [ ] 1281 NURSE SALLY'S LAST CHANCE Anne Durham
- [ ] 1304 SHARLIE FOR SHORT
       Dorothy Rivers
- [ ] 1317 BELOVED SPARROW
       Henrietta Reid
- [ ] 1353 NURSE LAVINIA'S MISTAKE
       Marjorie Norrell
- [ ] 1360 THIS DESIRABLE RESIDENCE
       Hilda Nickson
- [ ] 1370 THE WAYS OF LOVE
       Catherine Airlie
- [ ] 1378 NURSE SMITH, COOK
       Joyce Dingwell
- [ ] 1381 MUSIC ON THE WIND
       Dorothy Slide

All books are 60c. Please use the handy order coupon.

HH